CW01550006

THE COMPLETE HESIOD COLLECTION
BY

Hesiod

Translated by Hugh G. Evelyn-White

The Complete Hesiod Collection

The Shield of Heracles

Lines 1-38

Or like her who left home and country and came to Thebes, following warlike Amphitryon,— even Alcmena, the daughter of Electryon, gatherer of the people. She surpassed the tribe of womankind [5] in beauty and in height; and in wisdom none vied with her of those whom mortal women bore of union with mortal men. Her face and her dark eyes wafted such charm as comes from golden Aphrodite. And she so honored her husband in her heart [10] as none of womankind did before her. In truth he had slain her noble father violently when he was angry about oxen; so he left his own country and came to Thebes and was suppliant to the shield-carrying men of Cadmus. There he dwelt with his modest wife [15] without the joys of love, nor might he go in unto the neat-ankled daughter of Electryon until he had avenged the death of his wife's great-hearted brothers and utterly burned with blazing fire the villages of the heroes, the Taphians and Teleboans; [20] for this thing was laid upon him, and the gods were witnesses to it. And he feared their anger, and hastened to perform the great task to which Zeus had bound him. With him went the horse-driving Boeotians, breathing above their shields, [25] and the Locrians who fight hand to hand, and the gallant Phocians eager for war and battle. And the noble son of Alcaeus led them, rejoicing in his host. But the father of men and gods was forming another scheme in his heart, to beget one to defend against destruction gods and men who eat bread. [30] So he arose from Olympus by night pondering guile in the deep of his heart, and yearned for the love of the well-girded woman. Quickly he came to Typhaonium, and from there again wise Zeus went on and trod the highest peak of Phicium:[1] there he sat and planned marvellous things in his heart. [35] So in one night Zeus shared the bed and love of the neat-ankled daughter of Electryon and fulfilled his desire; and in the same night Amphitryon, gatherer of the people, the glorious hero, came to his house when he had ended his great task.

1 A mountain peak near Thebes which took its name from the Sphinx (called in **Hes. Th. 326** φῖξ) .

He hastened not to go to his bondmen and shepherds afield, [40] but first went in to his wife: such desire took hold on the shepherd of the people. And as a man who has escaped joyfully from misery, whether of sore disease or cruel bondage, so then did Amphitryon, when he had wound up all his heavy task, [45] come glad and welcome to his home. And all night long he lay with his modest wife, delighting in the gifts of golden Aphrodite. And she, being subject in love to a god and to a man exceeding goodly, brought forth twin sons in seven-gated Thebes. [50] Though they were brothers, these were not of one spirit; for one was weaker but the other a far better man, one terrible and strong, the mighty Heracles. She bore him through the embrace of the son of Cronos lord of dark clouds and the other, Iphicles, of Amphitryon the spear-wielder— [55] offspring distinct, this one of union with a mortal man, but that other of union with Zeus, leader of all the gods. And he slew Cycnus, the gallant son of Ares. For he found him in the precinct of far-shooting Apollo, him and his father Ares, never sated with war. [60] Their armour shone like a flame of blazing fire as they two stood in their chariot: their swift horses struck the earth and pawed it with their hoofs, and the dust rose like smoke about them, pounded by the chariot wheels and the horses' hoofs, while the well-made chariot and its rails rattled around them [65] as the horses plunged. And blameless Cycnus was glad, for he hoped to slay the warlike son of Zeus and his charioteer with the sword, and to strip off their splendid armour. But Phoebus Apollo would not listen to his vaunts, for he himself had stirred up mighty Heracles against him. [70] And all the grove and altar of Pagasaean Apollo flamed because of the dread god and because of his arms; for his eyes flashed as with fire. What mortal man would have dared to meet him face to face save Heracles and glorious Iolaus? [75] For great was their strength and unconquerable were the arms which grew from their shoulders on their strong limbs. Then Heracles spake to his charioteer strong Iolaus:

"O hero Iolaus, best beloved of all men, truly Amphitryon sinned deeply against the blessed gods who dwell on Olympus [80] when he came to sweet-crowned Thebes and left Tiryns, the well-built citadel, because he slew Electryon for the sake of his wide-browed oxen. Then he came to Creon and long-robed Eniocha, who received him kindly and gave him all fitting things, [85] as is due to suppliants, and honored him in their hearts even more. And he lived joyfully with his wife the neat-ankled daughter of Electryon: and presently, while the years rolled on, we were born, unlike in body as in mind, even your father and I. From him Zeus took away sense, so that he left his home and his parents [90] and went to do honor to the wicked Eurystheus— unhappy man! Deeply indeed did he grieve afterwards in bearing the burden of his own mad folly; but that cannot be taken back. But on me fate laid heavy tasks. [95] "Yet, come, friend, quickly take the red-dyed reins of the swift horses and raise high courage in your heart and guide the swift chariot and strong fleet-footed horses straight on. Have no secret fear at the noise of man-slaying Ares who now rages shouting about the holy grove [100] of Phoebus Apollo, the lord who shoots from afar. Surely, strong though he be, he will have enough of war." And blameless Iolaus answered him again: "Good friend, truly the father of men and gods greatly honors your head and the bull-like Earth-Shaker also, [105] who keeps Thebe's veil of walls and guards the city,—so great and strong is this fellow they bring into your hands that you may win great glory. But come, put on your arms of war that with all speed we may bring the car of Ares and our own together and [110] fight; for he shall not frighten the dauntless son of Zeus, nor yet the son of Iphiclus: rather I think he will flee before the two sons of blameless Alcides who are near him and eager to raise the war cry for battle; for this they love better than a feast."

So he said. And mighty Heracles was glad in heart and smiled, for the other's words pleased him well, and he answered him with winged words: "O hero Iolaus, heaven-sprung, now is rough battle hard at hand. [120] But, as you have shown your skill at other times, so now also wheel the great black-maned horse Arion about every way, and help me as you may be able." So he said, and put upon his legs greaves of shining bronze, the splendid gift of Hephaestus. Next he fastened about his breast [125] a fine golden breast-plate, curiously wrought, which Pallas Athena the daughter of Zeus had given him when first he was about to set out upon his grievous labors. Over his shoulders the fierce warrior put the steel that saves men from doom, and across his breast [130] he slung behind him a hollow quiver. Within it were many chilling arrows, dealers of death which makes speech forgotten: in front they had death, and trickled with tears; their shafts were smooth and very long; and their butts were covered with feathers of a brown eagle. [135] And he took his strong spear, pointed with shining bronze, and on his valiant head set a well-made helm of adamant, cunningly wrought, which fitted closely on the temples; and that guarded the head of god-like Heracles. In his hands he took his shield, all glittering: no one ever [140] broke it with a blow or crushed it. And a wonder it was to see; for its whole orb shimmered with enamel and white ivory and electrum, and it glowed with shining gold; and there were zones of cyanus[1] drawn upon it. In the center was Fear worked in adamant, unspeakable, [145] staring backwards with eyes that glowed with fire. His mouth was full of teeth in a white row, fearful and daunting, and upon his grim brow hovered frightful Strife who arrays the throng of men: pitiless she, for she took away the mind and senses of poor wretches [150] who made war against the son of Zeus. Their souls passed beneath the earth and went down into the house of Hades; but their bones, when the skin is rotted about them, crumble away on the dark earth under parching Sirius.

1 Cyanus was a glass-paste of deep blue color: the "zones" were concentric bands in which were the scenes described by the poet. The figure of Fear （1.44） occupied the center of the shield, and Oceanus （1.314） enclosed the whole.

Lines 154-177

Upon the shield Pursuit and Flight were wrought, [155] and Tumult, and Panic, and Slaughter. Strife also, and Uproar were hurrying about, and deadly Fate was there holding one man newly wounded, and another unwounded; and one, who was dead, she was dragging by the feet through the tumult. She had on her shoulders a garment red with the blood of men, [160] and terribly she glared and gnashed her teeth. And there were heads of snakes unspeakably frightful, twelve of them; and they used to frighten the tribes of men on earth made war against the son of Zeus; for they would clash their teeth when Amphitryon's son was fighting: [165] and brightly shone these wonderful works. And it was as though there were spots upon the frightful snakes: and their backs were dark blue and their jaws were black. Also there were upon the shield droves of boars and lions who glared at each other, being furious and eager: [170] the rows of them moved on together, and neither side trembled but both bristled up their manes. For already a great lion lay between them and two boars, one on either side, bereft of life, and their dark blood was dripping down upon the ground; [175] they lay dead with necks outstretched beneath the grim lions. And both sides were roused still more to fight because they were angry, the fierce boars and the bright-eyed lions.

And there was the strife of the Lapith spearmen gathered round the prince Caeneus and Dryas and Peirithous, [180] with Hopleus, Exadius, Phalereus, and Prolochus, Mopsus the son of Ampyce of Titaresia, a scion of Ares, and Theseus, the son of Aegeus, like the deathless gods. These were of silver, and had armor of gold upon their bodies. And the Centaurs were gathered against them on the other side [185] with Petraeus and Asbolus the diviner, Arctus, and Ureus, and black-haired Mimas, and the two sons of Peuceus, Perimedes and Dryalus: these were of silver, and they had pinetrees of gold in their hands, and they were rushing together as though they were alive [190] and striking at one another hand to hand with spears and with pines. And on the shield stood the fleet-footed horses of grim Ares made of gold, and deadly Ares the spoil-winner himself. He held a spear in his hands and was urging on the footmen: he was red with blood as if he were slaying living men, [195] and he stood in his chariot. Beside him stood Fear and Flight, eager to plunge amidst the fighting men. There, too, was the daughter of Zeus, Tritogeneia who drives the spoil. ¹She was like as if she would array a battle, with a spear in her hand, and a golden helmet, [200] and the aegis about her shoulders. And she was going towards the awful strife. And there was the holy company of the deathless gods: and in the midst the son of Zeus and Leto played sweetly on a golden lyre. There also was the abode of the gods, pure Olympus, and their assembly, and infinite riches were spread around [205] in the gathering of the deathless gods. Also the goddesses, the Muses of Pieria were beginning a song like clear-voiced singers. And on the shield was a harbor with a safe haven from the irresistible sea, made of refined tin wrought in a circle, and it seemed to heave with waves. In the middle of it were [210] many dolphins rushing this way and that, fishing: and they seemed to be swimming. Two dolphins of silver were spouting and devouring the mute fishes. And beneath them fishes of bronze were trembling. And on the shore sat a fisherman watching: in his hands he held [215] a casting net for fish, and seemed as if about to cast it forth.

1 "She who drives herds,"*i.e.*"The Victorious," since herds were the chief spoil gained by the victor in ancient warfare.

Lines 216-244

 There, too, was the son of rich-haired Danae, the horseman Perseus: his feet did not touch the shield and yet were not far from it—very marvellous to remark, since he was not supported anywhere; for so did the famous Lame One fashion him of gold with his hands. [220] On his feet he had winged sandals, and his black-sheathed sword was slung across his shoulders by a cross-belt of bronze. He was flying swift as thought. The head of a dreadful monster, the Gorgon, covered the broad of his back, and a bag of silver—a marvel to see— [225] contained it: and from the bag bright tassels of gold hung down. Upon the head of the hero lay the dread cap[1] of Hades which had the awful gloom of night. Perseus himself, the son of Danae, was at full stretch, like one who hurries and shudders with horror. And after him rushed [230] the Gorgons, unapproachable and unspeakable, longing to seize him: as they trod upon the pale adamant, the shield rang sharp and clear with a loud clanging. Two serpents hung down at their girdles with heads curved forward: [235] their tongues were flickering, and their teeth gnashing with fury, and their eyes glaring fiercely. And upon the awful heads of the Gorgons great Fear was quaking. And beyond these there were men fighting in warlike harness, some defending their own town and parents [240] from destruction, and others eager to sack it; many lay dead, but the greater number still strove and fought. The women on well-built towers of bronze were crying shrilly and tearing their cheeks like living beings—the work of famous Hephaestus.

 1 The cap of darkness which made its wearer invisible.

Lines 245-279

And the men who were elders and on whom age had laid hold were all together outside the gates, and were holding up their hands to the blessed gods, fearing for their own sons. But these again were engaged in battle: and behind them the dusky Fates, gnashing their white fangs, [250] lowering, grim, bloody, and unapproachable, struggled for those who were falling, for they all were longing to drink dark blood. So soon as they caught a man overthrown or falling newly wounded, one of them would clasp her great claws about him, and his soul would go down to Hades [255] to chilly Tartarus. And when they had satisfied their souls with human blood, they would cast that one behind them, and rush back again into the tumult and the fray. Clotho and Lachesis were over them and Atropos less tall than they, a goddess of no great frame, yet [260] superior to the others and the eldest of them. And they all made a fierce fight over one poor wretch, glaring evilly at one another with furious eyes and fighting equally with claws and hands. By them stood Darkness of Death, mournful and fearful, [265] pale, shrivelled, shrunk with hunger, swollen-kneed. Long nails tipped her hands, and she dribbled at the nose, and from her cheeks blood dripped down to the ground. She stood leering hideously, and much dust sodden with tears lay upon her shoulders. [270] Next, there was a city of men with goodly towers; and seven gates of gold, fitted to the lintels, guarded it. The men were making merry with festivities and dances; some were bringing home a bride to her husband on a well-wheeled car, while the bridalsong swelled high, [275] and the glow of blazing torches held by handmaidens rolled in waves afar. And these maidens went before, delighting in the festival; and after them came frolicsome choirs, the youths singing soft-mouthed to the sound of shrill pipes, while the echo was shivered around them, and the girls led on the lovely dance to the sound of lyres. Then again on the other side was a rout of young men revelling, with flutes playing; some frolicking with dance and song, and others were going forward in time with a flute player and laughing. The whole town was filled with mirth and dance and festivity. [285] Others again were mounted on horseback and galloping before the town. And there were ploughmen breaking up the good soil, clothed in tunics girt up. Also there was a wide cornland, and some men were reaping with sharp hooks the stalks [290] which bended with the weight of the ears—as if they were reaping Demeter's grain: others were binding the sheaves with bands and were spreading the threshing floor. And some held reaping hooks and were gathering the vintage, while others were taking from the reapers into baskets white and black clusters from the long rows of vines [295] which were heavy with leaves and tendrils of silver. Others again were gathering them into baskets. Beside them was a row of vines [297] in gold, the splendid work of cunning Hephaestus: [299] it had shivering leaves and stakes of silver [300] and was laden with grapes which turned black.[1] And there were men treading out the grapes and others drawing off the liquor. Also there were men boxing and wrestling, and huntsmen chasing swift hares with a leash of sharp-toothed dogs before them, they eager to catch the hares, and the hares eager to escape. [305] Next to them were horsemen hard set, and they contended and labored for a prize. The charioteers standing on their well-woven cars, urged on their swift horses with loose rein; the jointed cars flew along clattering and the naves of the wheels shrieked loudly. [310] So they were engaged in an unending toil, and the end with victory came never to them, and the contest was ever unwon. And there was set out for them within the course a great tripod of gold, the splendid work of cunning Hephaestus. And round the rim Ocean was flowing, with a full stream as it seemed, [315] and enclosed all the cunning work of the shield. Over it swans were soaring and calling loudly, and many others were swimming upon the surface of the water; and near them were shoals of fish. A wonderful thing the great strong shield was to see—even for Zeus the loud-thunderer, by whose will Hephaestus made it [320] and fitted it with his hands. This shield the valiant son of Zeus wielded masterly, and leaped upon his horse-chariot like the lightning of his father Zeus who holds the aegis, moving lithely. And his charioteer, strong Iolaus, standing upon the car, guided the curved chariot. [325] Then the goddess grey-eyed Athena came near them and spoke winged words, encouraging them:

1 The existing text of the vineyard scene is a compound of two different versions, clumsily adapted, and eked out with some makeshift additions.

"Hail, offspring of far-famed Lynceus! Even now Zeus who reigns over the blessed gods gives you power to slay Cycnus and to strip off his splendid armor. [330] Yet I will tell you something besides, mightiest of the people. When you have robbed Cycnus of sweet life, then leave him there and his armor also, and you yourself watch man-slaying Ares narrowly as he attacks, and wherever you shall see him uncovered below his cunningly-wrought shield, [335] there wound him with your sharp spear. Then draw back; for it is not ordained that you should take his horses or his splendid armor." So said the bright-eyed goddess and swiftly got up into the car with victory and renown in her hands. [340] Then heaven-nurtured Iolaus called terribly to the horses, and at his cry they swiftly whirled the fleet chariot along, raising dust from the plain; for the goddess bright-eyed Athena put mettle into them by shaking her aegis. And the earth groaned all round them. [345] And they, horse-taming Cycnus and Ares, insatiable in war, came on together like fire or whirlwind. Then their horses neighed shrilly, face to face; and the echo was shivered all round them. And mighty Heracles spoke first and said to that other: [350] "Cycnus, my friend! Why do you set your swift horses at us, men who are tried in labor and pain? No, guide your fleet car aside and yield and go out of the path. It is to Trachis I am driving on, to Ceyx the king, who is the first in Trachis for power and for honor, [355] and that you yourself know well, for you have his daughter dark-eyed Themistinoe to wife. Fool! For Ares shall not deliver you from the end of death, if we two meet together in battle. Another time ere this I declare he has made trial [360] of my spear, when he defended sandy Pylos and stood against me, fiercely longing for fight. Thrice was he stricken by my spear and dashed to earth, and his shield was pierced; but the fourth time I struck his thigh, laying on with all my strength, and tore deep into his flesh.

And he fell headlong in the dust upon the ground through the force of my spear-thrust; then truly he would have been disgraced among the deathless gods, if by my hands he had left behind his bloody spoils." So said he. But Cycnus the stout spearman cared not to obey him and to pull up the horses that drew his chariot. [370] Then it was that from their well-woven chariots they both leaped straight to the ground, the son of Zeus and the son of the Lord of War. The charioteers drove near by their horses with beautiful manes, and the wide earth rang with the beat of their hoofs as they rushed along. As when rocks leap forth from the high peak of a great mountain, [375] and fall on one another, and many towering oaks and pines and long-rooted poplars are broken by them as they whirl swiftly down until they reach the plain; so did they fall on one another with a great shout: [380] and all the town of the Myrmidons, and famous Iolcus, and Arne, and Helice, and grassy Anthea echoed loudly at the voice of the two. With an awful cry they closed: and wise Zeus thundered loudly and rained down drops of blood, [385] giving the signal for battle to his dauntless son. As a tusked boar, fearful for a man to see before him in the glens of a mountain, resolves to fight with the huntsmen and whets his white tusks, turning sideways, while foam flows all round his mouth [390] as he gnashes, and his eyes are like glowing fire, and he bristles the hair on his mane and around his neck—, like him the son of Zeus leaped from his horse chariot. And when the dark-winged whirring grasshopper, perched on a green shoot, begins to sing of summer to men— [395] his food and drink is the dainty dew— and all day long from dawn pours forth his voice in the deadliest heat, when Sirius scorches the flesh   (then the beard grows upon the millet which men sow in summer) , when the crude grapes [400] which Dionysus gave to men— a joy and a sorrow both—begin to color, in that season they fought and loud rose the clamor.

As two lions[1] on either side of a slain deer spring at one another in fury, and there is a fearful snarling and a clashing also of teeth—, [405] like vultures with crooked talons and hooked beak that fight and scream aloud on a high rock over a mountain goat or fat wild-deer which some active man has shot with an arrow from the string, and himself has wandered away elsewhere, [410] not knowing the place; but they quickly mark it and vehemently do keen battle about it—, like these they two rushed upon one another with a shout. Then Cycnus, eager to kill the son of almighty Zeus, struck upon his shield with a brazen spear, [415] but did not break the bronze; and the gift of the god saved his foe. But the son of Amphitryon, mighty Heracles, with his long spear struck Cycnus violently in the neck beneath the chin, where it was unguarded between helm and shield. And the deadly spear cut through the two sinews; [420] for the hero's full strength lighted on his foe. And Cycnus fell as an oak falls or a lofty pine that is stricken by the lurid thunderbolt of Zeus; even so he fell, and his armour adorned with bronze clashed about him. Then the stout-hearted son of Zeus let him be, [425] and himself watched for the onset of manslaying Ares: fiercely he stared, like a lion who has come upon a body and full eagerly rips the hide with his strong claws and takes away the sweet life with all speed: his dark heart is filled with rage [430] and his eyes glare fiercely, while he tears up the earth with his paws and lashes his flanks and shoulders with his tail so that no one dares to face him and go near to give battle. Even so, the son of Amphitryon, unsated of battle, stood eagerly face to face with Ares, [435] nursing courage in his heart. And Ares drew near him with grief in his heart; and they both sprang at one another with a cry. As it is when a rock shoots out from a great cliff and whirls down with long bounds, careering eagerly with a roar, and a high crag clashes with it and keeps it there where they strike together; [440] with no less clamor did deadly Ares, the chariot-borne, rush shouting at Heracles. And he quickly received the attack.

1 The conception is similar to that of the sculptured group at Athens of Two Lions devouring a Bull (Dickens,*Cat. of the Acropolis Museum,*No. 3) .

Lines 433-End

But Athena the daughter of aegis-bearing Zeus came to meet Ares, wearing the dark aegis, [445] and she looked at him with an angry frown and spoke winged words to him. "Ares, check your fierce anger and matchless hands; for it is not ordained that you should kill Heracles, the bold-hearted son of Zeus, and strip off his rich armor. Come, then, cease fighting and do not withstand me." [450] So said she, but did not move the courageous spirit of Ares. But he uttered a great shout and waving his spears like fire, he rushed headlong at strong Heracles, longing to kill him, and hurled a brazen spear upon the great shield, for he was furiously angry because of his dead son; [455] but bright-eyed Athena reached out from the chariot and turned aside the force of the spear. Then bitter grief seized Ares, and he drew his keen sword and leaped upon bold-hearted Heracles. But as he came on, the son of Amphitryon, unsated of fierce battle, [460] shrewdly wounded his thigh where it was exposed under his richly-wrought shield, and tore deep into his flesh with the spear thrust and cast him flat upon the ground. And Panic and Dread quickly drove his smooth-wheeled chariot and horses near him and lifted him from the wide-pathed earth [465] into his richly-wrought car, and then straight lashed the horses and came to high Olympus. But the son of Alcmena and glorious Iolaus stripped the fine armour off Cycnus' shoulders and went, [470] and their swift horses carried them straight to the city of Trachis. And bright-eyed Athena went from there to great Olympus and her father's house. As for Cycnus, Ceyx buried him and the countless people who lived near the city of the glorious king, in Anthe and the city of the Myrmidons, and famous Iolcus, [475] and Arne, and Helice: and many people were gathered doing honor to Ceyx, the friend of the blessed gods. But Anaurus, swelled by a rain-storm, blotted out the grave and memorial of Cycnus; for so Apollo, Leto's son, commanded him, because he used to watch for and violently despoil the rich hecatombs [480] that any might bring to Phyto.

Theogony

Lines 1- 28

From the Heliconian Muses let us begin to sing, who hold the great and holy mount of Helicon, and dance on soft feet about the deep-blue spring and the altar of the almighty son of Cronos, [5] and, when they have washed their tender bodies in Permessus or in the Horse's Spring or Olmeius, make their fair, lovely dances upon highest Helicon and move with vigorous feet. Thence they arise and go abroad by night, [10] veiled in thick mist, and utter their song with lovely voice, praising Zeus the aegis-holder, and queenly Hera of Argos who walks on golden sandals, and the daughter of Zeus the aegis-holder bright-eyed Athena, and Phoebus Apollo, and Artemis who delights in arrows, [15] and Poseidon the earth holder who shakes the earth, and revered Themis, and quick-glancing¹Aphrodite, and Hebe with the crown of gold, and fair Dione, Leto, Iapetus, and Cronos the crafty counsellor, Eos, and great Helius, and bright Selene, [20] Earth, too, and great Oceanus, and dark Night, and the holy race of all the other deathless ones that are for ever. And one day they taught Hesiod glorious song while he was shepherding his lambs under holy Helicon, and this word first the goddesses said to me— [25] the Muses of Olympus, daughters of Zeus who holds the aegis: "Shepherds of the wilderness, wretched things of shame, mere bellies, we know how to speak many false things as though they were true; but we know, when we will, to utter true things."

1 The epithet probably indicates coquettishness.

Lines 29-52

So said the ready-voiced daughters of great Zeus, and they plucked and gave [30] me a rod, a shoot of sturdy laurel, a marvellous thing, and breathed into me a divine voice to celebrate things that shall be and things that were aforetime; and they bade me sing of the race of the blessed gods that are eternally, but ever to sing of themselves both first and last. [35] But why all this about oak or stone?¹ Come you, let us begin with the Muses who gladden the great spirit of their father Zeus in Olympus with their songs, telling of things that are and that shall be and that were aforetime with consenting voice. Unwearying flows the sweet sound [40] from their lips, and the house of their father Zeus the loud-thunderer is glad at the lily-like voice of the goddesses as it spreads abroad, and the peaks of snowy Olympus resound, and the homes of the immortals. And they, uttering their immortal voice, celebrate in song first of all the revered race of the gods [45] from the beginning, those whom Earth and wide Heaven begot, and the gods sprung of these, givers of good things. Then next, the goddesses sing of Zeus, the father of gods and men, as they begin and end their strain, how much he is the most excellent among the gods and supreme in power. [50] And again, they chant the race of men and strong giants, and gladden the heart of Zeus within Olympus,—the Olympian Muses, daughters of Zeus the aegis-holder.

1 A proverbial saying meaning, "why enlarge on irrelevant topics?"

Lines 53-62

   Them in Pieria did Mnemosyne （Memory）, who reigns over the hills of Eleuther, bear of union with the father, the son of Cronos, [55] a forgetting of ills and a rest from sorrow. For nine nights did wise Zeus lie with her, entering her holy bed remote from the immortals. And when a year was passed and the seasons came round as the months waned, and many days were accomplished, [60] she bore nine daughters, all of one mind, whose hearts are set upon song, and whose spirit is free from care, a little way from the top-most peak of snowy Olympus.

Lines 63-103

There are their bright dancing places and beautiful homes, and beside them the Graces and Himerus (Desire) live [65] in delight. And they, uttering through their lips a lovely voice, sing the laws of all and the goodly ways of the immortals, uttering their lovely voice. Then went they to Olympus, delighting in their sweet voice, with heavenly song, and the dark earth resounded [70] about them as they chanted and a lovely sound rose up beneath their feet as they went to their father. And he was reigning in heaven, himself holding the lightning and glowing thunderbolt, when he had overcome by might his father Cronos; and he distributed fairly to the immortals their portions and declared their privileges. [75] These things, then, the Muses sang who dwell on Olympus, nine daughters begotten by great Zeus, Cleio and Euterpe, Thaleia, Melpomene and Terpsichore, and Erato and Polyhymnia and Urania and Calliope,[1] who is the chiefest of them all, [80] for she attends on worshipful princes: whomever of heaven-nourished princes the daughters of great Zeus honor and behold at his birth, they pour sweet dew upon his tongue, and from his lips flow gracious words. All the people [85] look towards him while he settles causes with true judgements: and he, speaking surely, would soon make wise end even of a great quarrel; for therefore are there princes wise in heart, because when the people are being misguided in their assembly, they set right the matter again [90] with ease, persuading them with gentle words. And when he passes through a gathering, they greet him as a god with gentle reverence, and he is conspicuous amongst the assembled: such is the holy gift of the Muses to men. For it is through the Muses and far-shooting Apollo that [95] there are singers and harpers upon the earth; but princes are of Zeus, and happy is he whom the Muses love: sweet flows speech from his mouth. For although a man has sorrow and grief in his newly-troubled soul and lives in dread because his heart is distressed, yet, when a singer, [100] the servant of the Muses, chants the glorious deeds of men of old and the blessed gods who inhabit Olympus, at once he forgets his heaviness and remembers not his sorrows at all; but the gifts of the goddesses soon turn him away from these.

1 "She of the noble voice." Calliope is queen of Epic poetry.

Lines 104-138

Hail, children of Zeus! Grant lovely song [105] and celebrate the holy race of the deathless gods who are for ever, those that were born of Earth and starry Heaven and gloomy Night and them that briny Sea did rear. Tell how at the first gods and earth came to be, and rivers, and the boundless sea with its raging swell, [110] and the gleaming stars, and the wide heaven above, and the gods who were born of them, givers of good things, and how they divided their wealth, and how they shared their honors amongst them, and also how at the first they took many-folded Olympus. These things declare to me from the beginning, you Muses who dwell in the house of Olympus, [115] and tell me which of them first came to be. In truth at first Chaos came to be, but next wide-bosomed Earth, the ever-sure foundation of all[1]the deathless ones who hold the peaks of snowy Olympus, and dim Tartarus in the depth of the wide-pathed Earth, [120] and Eros

(Love) , fairest among the deathless gods, who unnerves the limbs and overcomes the mind and wise counsels of all gods and all men within them. From Chaos came forth Erebus and black Night; but of Night were born Aether[2]and Day, [125] whom she conceived and bore from union in love with Erebus. And Earth first bore starry Heaven, equal to herself, to cover her on every side, and to be an ever-sure abiding-place for the blessed gods. And she brought forth long hills, graceful haunts [130] of the goddess Nymphs who dwell amongst the glens of the hills. She bore also the fruitless deep with his raging swell, Pontus, without sweet union of love. But afterwards she lay with Heaven and bore deep-swirling Oceanus, Coeus and Crius and Hyperion and Iapetus, [135] Theia and Rhea, Themis and Mnemosyne and gold-crowned Phoebe and lovely Tethys. After them was born Cronos the wily, youngest and most terrible of her children, and he hated his lusty sire.

1 Earth, in the cosmology of Hesiod, is a disk surrounded by the river Oceanus and floating upon a waste of waters. It is called the foundation of all (the qualification "the deathless ones..." etc. is an interpolation) , because not only trees, men, and animals, but even the hills and seas (ll. 129, 131) are supported by it.

2 Aether is the bright, untainted upper atmosphere, as distinguished from Aer, the lower atmosphere of the earth.

Lines 139-172

And again, she bore the Cyclopes, overbearing in spirit, [140] Brontes, and Steropes and stubborn-hearted Arges,[1] who gave Zeus the thunder and made the thunderbolt: in all else they were like the gods, [145] but one eye only was set in the midst of their foreheads. And they were surnamed Cyclopes (Orb-eyed) because one orbed eye was set in their foreheads. Strength and might and craft were in their works. And again, three other sons were born of Earth and Heaven, great and doughty beyond telling, Cottus and Briareos and Gyes, presumptuous children. [150] From their shoulders sprang a hundred arms, not to be approached, and fifty heads grew from the shoulders upon the strong limbs of each, and irresistible was the stubborn strength that was in their great forms. For of all the children that were born of Earth and Heaven, [155] these were the most terrible, and they were hated by their own father from the first. And he used to hide them all away in a secret place of Earth so soon as each was born, and would not suffer them to come up into the light: and Heaven rejoiced in his evil doing. But vast Earth [160] groaned within, being straitened, and she thought a crafty and an evil wile. Forthwith she made the element of grey flint and shaped a great sickle, and told her plan to her dear sons. And she spoke, cheering them, while she was vexed in her dear heart: [165] "My children, gotten of a sinful father, if you will obey me, we should punish the vile outrage of your father; for he first thought of doing shameful things." So she said; but fear seized them all, and none of them uttered a word. But great Cronos the wily took courage and answered his dear mother: [170] "Mother, I will undertake to do this deed, for I reverence not our father of evil name, for he first thought of doing shameful things."

1 Brontes is the Thunderer; Steropes, the Lightning Flash; and Arges, the Vivid One.

Lines 173-206

So he said: and vast Earth rejoiced greatly in spirit, and set and hid him in an ambush, and put in his hands [175] a jagged sickle, and revealed to him the whole plot. And Heaven came, bringing on night and longing for love, and he lay about Earth spreading himself full upon her.[1]Then the son from his ambush stretched forth his left hand and in his right took the great long sickle [180] with jagged teeth, and swiftly lopped off his own father's members and cast them away to fall behind him. And not vainly did they fall from his hand; for all the bloody drops that gushed forth Earth received, and as the seasons moved round [185] she bore the strong Erinyes and the great Giants with gleaming armour, holding long spears in their hands and the Nymphs whom they call Meliae[2]all over the boundless earth. And so soon as he had cut off the members with flint and cast them from the land into the surging sea, [190] they were swept away over the main a long time: and a white foam spread around them from the immortal flesh, and in it there grew a maiden. First she drew near holy Cythera, and from there, afterwards, she came to sea-girt Cyprus, and came forth an awful and lovely goddess, and grass [195] grew up about her beneath her shapely feet. Her gods and men call Aphrodite, and the foam-born goddess and rich-crowned Cytherea, because she grew amid the foam, and Cytherea because she reached Cythera, and Cyprogenes because she was born in billowy Cyprus, [200] and Philommedes[3] because she sprang from the members. And with her went Eros, and comely Desire followed her at her birth at the first and as she went into the assembly of the gods. This honor she has from the beginning, and this is the portion allotted to her amongst men and undying gods,— [205] the whisperings of maidens and smiles and deceits with sweet delight and love and graciousness.

1 The myth accounts for the separation of Heaven and Earth. In Egyptian cosmology Nut (the Sky) is thrust and held apart from her brother Geb (the Earth) by their father Shu, who corresponds to the Greek Atlas.

2 Nymphs of the ash-trees (μέλιαι) , as Dryads are nymphs of the oak-trees. Cp. note onWorks and Days, l. 145.

3 "Member-loving": the title is perhaps only a perversion of the regularφιλομειδής (laughter-loving) .

But these sons whom he begot himself great Heaven used to call Titans (Strainers) in reproach, for he said that they strained and did presumptuously [210] a fearful deed, and that vengeance for it would come afterwards. And Night bore hateful Doom and black Fate and Death, and she bore Sleep and the tribe of Dreams. [214] And again the goddess murky Night, though she lay with none, [213] bare Blame and painful Woe, [215] and the Hesperides who guard the rich, golden apples and the trees bearing fruit beyond glorious Ocean. Also she bore the Destinies and ruthless avenging Fates, Clotho and Lachesis and Atropos,[1]who give men at their birth both evil and good to have, [220] and they pursue the transgressions of men and of gods: and these goddesses never cease from their dread anger until they punish the sinner with a sore penalty. Also deadly Night bore Nemesis (Indignation) to afflict mortal men, and after her, Deceit and Friendship [225] and hateful Age and hard-hearted Strife. But abhorred Strife bore painful Toil and Forgetfulness and Famine and tearful Sorrows, Fightings also, Battles, Murders, Manslaughters, Quarrels, Lying Words, Disputes, [230] Lawlessness and Ruin, all of one nature, and Oath who most troubles men upon earth when anyone willfully swears a false oath. And Sea begat Nereus, the eldest of his children, who is true and lies not: and men call him the Old Man [235] because he is trusty and gentle and does not forget the laws of righteousness, but thinks just and kindly thoughts. And yet again he got great Thaumas and proud Phorcys, being mated with Earth, and fair-cheeked Ceto and Eurybia who has a heart of flint within her.

1 Clotho (the Spinner) is she who spins the thread of man's life; Lachesis (the Disposer of Lots) assigns to each man his destiny; Atropos (She who cannot be turned) is the "Fury with the abhorre\d shears."

And of Nereus and rich-haired Doris, daughter of Ocean the perfect river, were born children,[1]passing lovely amongst goddesses, Ploto, Eucrante, Sao, and Amphitrite, and Eudora, and Thetis, Galene and Glauce, [245] Cymothoe, Speo, Thoe and lovely Halie, and Pasithea, and Erato, and rosy-armed Eunice, and gracious Melite, and Eulimene, and Agaue, Doto, Proto, Pherusa, and Dynamene, and Nisaea, and Actaea, and Protomedea, [250] Doris, Panopea, and comely Galatea, and lovely Hippothoe, and rosy-armed Hipponoe, and Cymodoce who with Cymatolege[2]and Amphitrite easily calms the waves upon the misty sea and the blasts of raging winds, [255] and Cymo, and Eione, and rich-crowned Alimede, and Glauconome, fond of laughter, and Pontoporea, Leagore, Euagore, and Laomedea, and Polynoe, and Autonoe, and Lysianassa, and Euarne, lovely of shape and without blemish of form, [260] and Psamathe of charming figure and divine Menippe, Neso, Eupompe, Themisto, Pronoe, and Nemertes[3]who has the nature of her deathless father. These fifty daughters sprang from blameless Nereus, skilled in excellent crafts. [265] And Thaumas wedded Electra the daughter of deep-flowing Ocean, and she bore him swift Iris and the long-haired Harpies, Aello (Storm-swift) and Ocypetes (Swift-flier) who on their swift wings keep pace with the blasts of the winds and the birds; for quick as time they dart along.

1 Many of the names which follow express various qualities or aspects of the sea: thus Galene is "Calm," Cymothoe is the "Wave-swift," Pherusa and Dynamene are "She who speeds (ships) " and "She who has power."

2 The "Wave-receiver" and the "Wave-stiller."

3 "The Unerring" or "Truthful"; cp. 1. 235.

Lines 270-303

And again, Ceto bore to Phorcys the fair-cheeked Graiae, sisters grey from their birth: and both deathless gods and men who walk on earth call them Graiae, Pemphredo well-clad, and saffron-robed Enyo, and the Gorgons who dwell beyond glorious Ocean [275] in the frontier land towards Night where are the clear-voiced Hesperides, Sthenno, and Euryale, and Medusa who suffered a woeful fate: she was mortal, but the two were undying and grew not old. With her lay the Dark-haired One[1] in a soft meadow amid spring flowers. [280] And when Perseus cut off her head, there sprang forth great Chrysaor and the horse Pegasus who is so called because he was born near the springs[2] of Ocean; and that other, because he held a golden blade[3] in his hands. Now Pegasus flew away and left the earth, the mother of flocks, [285] and came to the deathless gods: and he dwells in the house of Zeus and brings to wise Zeus the thunder and lightning. But Chrysaor was joined in love to Callirrhoe, the daughter of glorious Ocean, and begot three-headed Geryones. Him mighty Heracles slew [290] in sea-girt Erythea by his shambling oxen on that day when he drove the wide-browed oxen to holy Tiryns, and had crossed the ford of Ocean and killed Orthus and Eurytion the herdsman in the dim stead out beyond glorious Ocean. [300] And in a hollow cave she bore another monster, irresistible, in no wise like either to mortal men or to the undying gods, even the goddess fierce Echidna who is half a nymph with glancing eyes and fair cheeks, and half again a huge snake, great and awful, with speckled skin, eating raw flesh beneath the secret parts of the holy earth. And there she has a cave deep down under a hollow rock far from the deathless gods and mortal men. There, then, did the gods appoint her a glorious house to dwell in: and she keeps guard in Arima beneath the earth, grim Echidna, [305] a nymph who dies not nor grows old all her days.

1 i.e.Poseidon.

2 pegae

Lines 304-336

Men say that Typhaon the terrible, outrageous and lawless, was joined in love to her, the maid with glancing eyes. So she conceived and brought forth fierce offspring; first she bore Orthus the hound of Geryones, [310] and then again she bore a second, a monster not to be overcome and that may not be described, Cerberus who eats raw flesh, the brazen-voiced hound of Hades, fifty-headed, relentless and strong. And again she bore a third, the evil-minded Hydra of Lerna, whom the goddess, white-armed Hera nourished, [315] being angry beyond measure with the mighty Heracles. And her Heracles, the son of Zeus, of the house of Amphitryon, together with warlike Iolaus, destroyed with the unpitying sword through the plans of Athena the spoil driver. She was the mother of Chimaera who breathed raging fire, [320] a creature fearful, great, swift footed and strong, who had three heads, one of a grim-eyed lion, another of a goat, and another of a snake, a fierce dragon; in her forepart she was a lion; in her hinderpart, a dragon; and in her middle, a goat, breathing forth a fearful blast of blazing fire. [325] Her did Pegasus and noble Bellerophon slay; but Echidna was subject in love to Orthus and brought forth the deadly Sphinx which destroyed the Cadmeans, and the Nemean lion, which Hera, the good wife of Zeus, brought up and made to haunt the hills of Nemea, a plague to men. [330] There he preyed upon the tribes of her own people and had power over Tretus of Nemea and Apesas: yet the strength of stout Heracles overcame him. And Ceto was joined in love to Phorcys and bore her youngest, the awful snake who guards [335] the apples all of gold in the secret places of the dark earth at its great bounds. This is the offspring of Ceto and Phorcys.

Lines 337-370

And Tethys bore to Ocean eddying rivers, Nilus, and Alpheus, and deep-swirling Eridanus, Strymon, and Meander, and the fair stream of Ister, [340] and Phasis, and Rhesus, and the silver eddies of Achelous, Nessus, and Rhodius, Haliacmon, and Heptaporus, Granicus, and Aesepus, and holy Simois, and Peneus, and Hermus, and Caicus' fair stream, and great Sangarius, Ladon, Parthenius, [345] Euenus, Ardescus, and divine Scamander. Also she brought forth a holy company of daughters¹who with the lord Apollo and the Rivers have youths in their keeping—to this charge Zeus appointed them—Peitho, and Admete, and Ianthe, and Electra, [350] and Doris, and Prymno, and Urania divine in form, Hippo, Clymene, Rhodea, and Callirrhoe, Zeuxo and Clytie, and Idyia, and Pasithoe, Plexaura, and Galaxaura, and lovely Dione, Melobosis and Thoe and handsome Polydora, [355] Cerceis lovely of form, and soft eyed Pluto, Perseis, Ianeira, Acaste, Xanthe, Petraea the fair, Menestho, and Europa, Metis, and Eurynome, and Telesto saffron-clad, Chryseis and Asia and charming Calypso, [360] Eudora, and Tyche, Amphirho, and Ocyrrhoe, and Styx who is the chiefest of them all. These are the eldest daughters that sprang from Ocean and Tethys; but there are many besides. For there are three thousand neat-ankled daughters of Ocean who are dispersed far and wide, [365] and in every place alike serve the earth and the deep waters, children who are glorious among goddesses. And as many other rivers are there, babbling as they flow, sons of Ocean, whom queenly Tethys bare, but their names it is hard for a mortal man to tell, [370] but people know those by which they severally dwell.

1 Goettling notes that some of these nymphs derive their names from lands over which they preside, as Europa, Asia, Doris, Ianeira ("Lady of the Ionians") , but that most are called after some quality which their streams possessed: thus Xanthe is the "Brown" or "Turbid," Amphirho is the "Surrounding" river, Ianthe is "She who delights," and Ocyrrhoe is the "Swift-flowing."

Lines 371-403

And Theia was subject in love to Hyperion and bore great Helius (Sun) and clear Selene (Moon) and Eos (Dawn) who shines upon all that are on earth and upon the deathless Gods who live in the wide heaven. [375] And Eurybia, bright goddess, was joined in love to Crius and bore great Astraeus, and Pallas, and Perses who also was eminent among all men in wisdom. And Eos bore to Astraeus the strong-hearted winds, brightening Zephyrus, and Boreas, headlong in his course, [380] and Notus,—a goddess mating in love with a god. And after these Erigeneia[1] bare the star Eosphorus (Dawn-bringer) , and the gleaming stars with which heaven is crowned. And Styx the daughter of Ocean was joined to Pallas and bore Zelus (Emulation) and trim-ankled Nike (Victory) in the house. Also she brought forth [385] Cratos (Strength) and Bia (Force) , wonderful children. These have no house apart from Zeus, nor any dwelling nor path except that wherein God leads them, but they dwell always with Zeus the loud-thunderer. For so did Styx the deathless daughter of Ocean plan [390] on that day when the Olympian Lightning god called all the deathless gods to great Olympus, and said that whosoever of the gods would fight with him against the Titans, he would not cast him out from his rights, but each should have the office which he had before amongst the deathless gods. [395] And he declared that he who was without office or right under Cronos, should be raised to both office and rights as is just. So deathless Styx came first to Olympus with her children through the wit of her dear father. And Zeus honored her, and gave her very great gifts, [400] for he appointed her to be the great oath of the gods, and her children to live with him always. And as he promised, so he performed fully unto them all. But he himself mightily reigns and rules.

1 I.e.Eos, the "Early born."

Again, Phoebe came to the desired embrace of Coeus. [405] Then the goddess through the love of the god conceived and brought forth dark-gowned Leto, always mild, kind to men and to the deathless gods, mild from the beginning, gentlest in all Olympus. Also she bore Asteria of happy name, whom Perses once [410] led to his great house to be called his dear wife. And she conceived and bore Hecate whom Zeus the son of Cronos honored above all. He gave her splendid gifts, to have a share of the earth and the unfruitful sea. She received honor also in starry heaven, [415] and is honored exceedingly by the deathless gods. For to this day, whenever any one of men on earth offers rich sacrifices and prays for favor according to custom, he calls upon Hecate. Great honor comes full easily to him whose prayers the goddess receives favorably, [420] and she bestows wealth upon him; for the power surely is with her. For as many as were born of Earth and Ocean amongst all these she has her due portion. The son of Cronos did her no wrong nor took anything away of all that was her portion among the former Titan gods: [425] but she holds, as the division was at the first from the beginning, [427] privilege both in earth, and in heaven, and in sea. [426] Also, because she is an only child, the goddess receives not less honor, [428] but much more still, for Zeus honors her. Whom she will she greatly aids and advances: [434] she sits by worshipful kings in judgement, [430] and in the assembly whom she will is distinguished among the people. And when men arm themselves for the battle that destroys men, [433] then the goddess is at hand to give victory and grant glory readily to whom she will. [435] Good is she also when men contend at the games, for there too the goddess is with them and profits them: and he who by might and strength gets the victory wins the rich prize easily with joy, and brings glory to his parents. And she is good to stand by horsemen, whom she will: [440] and to those whose business is in the grey discomfortable sea, and who pray to Hecate and the loud-crashing Earth-Shaker, easily the glorious goddess gives great catch, and easily she takes it away as soon as seen, if so she will. She is good in the byre with Hermes to increase the stock. [445] The droves of kine and wide herds of goats and flocks of fleecy sheep, if she will, she increases from a few, or makes many to be less. So, then, albeit her mother's only child,[1]she is honored amongst all the deathless gods. [450] And the son of Cronos made her a nurse of the young who after that day saw with their eyes the light of all-seeing Dawn. So from the beginning she is a nurse of the young, and these are her honors.

1 Van Lennep explains that Hecate, having no brothers to support her claim, might have been slighted.

Lines 453-491

But Rhea was subject in love to Cronos and bore splendid children, Hestia,[1]Demeter, and gold-shod Hera [455] and strong Hades, pitiless in heart, who dwells under the earth, and the loud-crashing Earth-Shaker, and wise Zeus, father of gods and men, by whose thunder the wide earth is shaken. These great Cronos swallowed as each [460] came forth from the womb to his mother's knees with this intent, that no other of the proud sons of Heaven should hold the kingly office amongst the deathless gods. For he learned from Earth and starry Heaven that he was destined to be overcome by his own son, [465] strong though he was, through the contriving of great Zeus.[2]Therefore he kept no blind outlook, but watched and swallowed down his children: and unceasing grief seized Rhea. But when she was about to bear Zeus, the father of gods and men, [470] then she besought her own dear parents, Earth and starry Heaven, to devise some plan with her that the birth of her dear child might be concealed, and that retribution might overtake great, crafty Cronos for his own father and also for the children whom he had swallowed down. And they readily heard and obeyed their dear daughter, [475] and told her all that was destined to happen touching Cronos the king and his stout-hearted son. So they sent her to Lyctus, to the rich land of Crete, when she was ready to bear great Zeus, the youngest of her children. Him did vast Earth receive from Rhea [480] in wide Crete to nourish and to bring up. To that place came Earth carrying him swiftly through the black night to Lyctus first, and took him in her arms and hid him in a remote cave beneath the secret places of the holy earth on thick-wooded Mount Aegeum; but to the mightily ruling son of Heaven, the earlier king of the gods, [485] she gave a great stone wrapped in swaddling clothes. Then he took it in his hands and thrust it down into his belly: wretch! he knew not in his heart that in place of the stone his son was left behind, unconquered and untroubled, [490] and that he was soon to overcome him by force and might and drive him from his honors, himself to reign over the deathless gods.

1 The goddess of thehearth (the RomanVesta) , and so of the house. Cp.Homeric Hymnsv. 22 ff.; XXIX. 1 ff.

2 The variant reading "of his father" (sc.Heaven) rests on inferior MS. authority and is probably an alteration due to the difficulty stated by a Scholiast: "How could Zeus, being not yet begotten, plot against his father?" The phrase is, however, part of the prophecy. The whole line may well be spurious, and is rejected by Heyne, Wolf, Gaisford and Guyet.

Lines 492-506

After that, the strength and glorious limbs of the prince increased quickly, and as the years rolled on, great Cronos the wily was beguiled by the deep suggestions of Earth, [495] and brought up again his offspring, vanquished by the arts and might of his own son, and he vomited up first [500] the stone which he had swallowed last. And Zeus set it fast in the wide-pathed earth at goodly Pytho under the glens of Parnassus, to be a sign thenceforth and a marvel to mortal men.[1]And he set free from their deadly bonds the brothers of his father, sons of Heaven whom his father in his foolishness had bound. And they remembered to be grateful to him for his kindness, and gave him thunder and the glowing thunderbolt [505] and lightning: for before that, huge Earth had hidden these. In them he trusts and rules over mortals and immortals.

1 Pausanias (x.24.6) saw near the tomb of Neoptolemus "a stone of no great size," which the Delphians anointed every day with oil, and which he says was supposed to be the stone given to Cronos.

Lines 507-544

Now Iapetus took to wife the neat-ankled maid Clymene, daughter of Ocean, and went up with her into one bed. And she bore him a stout-hearted son, Atlas: [510] also she bore very glorious Menoetius and clever Prometheus, full of various wiles, and scatter-brained Epimetheus who from the first was a mischief to men who eat bread; for it was he who first took of Zeus the woman, the maiden whom he had formed. But Menoetius was outrageous, and farseeing Zeus [515] struck him with a lurid thunderbolt and sent him down to Erebus because of his mad presumption and exceeding pride. And Atlas through hard constraint upholds the wide heaven with unwearying head and arms, standing at the borders of the earth before the clear-voiced Hesperides; [520] for this lot wise Zeus assigned to him. And ready-witted Prometheus he bound with inextricable bonds, cruel chains, and drove a shaft through his middle, and set on him a long-winged eagle, which used to eat his immortal liver; but by night the liver grew [525] as much again everyway as the long-winged bird devoured in the whole day. That bird Heracles, the valiant son of shapely-ankled Alcmene, slew; and delivered the son of Iapetus from the cruel plague, and released him from his affliction—not without the will of Olympian Zeus who reigns on high, [530] that the glory of Heracles the Theban-born might be yet greater than it was before over the plenteous earth. This, then, he regarded, and honored his famous son; though he was angry, he ceased from the wrath which he had before because Prometheus matched himself in wit with the almighty son of Cronos. [535] For when the gods and mortal men had a dispute at Mecone, even then Prometheus was forward to cut up a great ox and set portions before them, trying to deceive the mind of Zeus. Before the rest he set flesh and inner parts thick with fat upon the hide, covering them with an ox paunch; [540] but for Zeus he put the white bones dressed up with cunning art and covered with shining fat. Then the father of men and of gods said to him: "Son of Iapetus, most glorious of all lords, good sir, how unfairly you have divided the portions!"

Lines 545-584

So said Zeus whose wisdom is everlasting, rebuking him. But wily Prometheus answered him, smiling softly and not forgetting his cunning trick: "Zeus, most glorious and greatest of the eternal gods, take which ever of these portions your heart within you bids." [550] So he said, thinking trickery. But Zeus, whose wisdom is everlasting, saw and failed not to perceive the trick, and in his heart he thought mischief against mortal men which also was to be fulfilled. With both hands he took up the white fat and was angry at heart, and wrath came to his spirit [555] when he saw the white ox-bones craftily tricked out: and because of this the tribes of men upon earth burn white bones to the deathless gods upon fragrant altars. But Zeus who drives the clouds was greatly vexed and said to him: "Son of Iapetus, clever above all! [560] So, sir, you have not yet forgotten your cunning arts!" So spake Zeus in anger, whose wisdom is everlasting; and from that time he was always mindful of the trick, and would not give the power of unwearying fire to the Melian[1] race of mortal men who live on the earth. [565] But the noble son of Iapetus outwitted him and stole the far-seen gleam of unwearying fire in a hollow fennel stalk. And Zeus who thunders on high was stung in spirit, and his dear heart was angered when he saw amongst men the far-seen ray of fire. [570] Forthwith he made an evil thing for men as the price of fire; for the very famous Limping God formed of earth the likeness of a shy maiden as the son of Cronos willed. And the goddess bright-eyed Athena girded and clothed her with silvery raiment, and down from her head [575] she spread with her hands an embroidered veil, a wonder to see; and she, Pallas Athena, put about her head lovely garlands, flowers of new-grown herbs. Also she put upon her head a crown of gold which the very famous Limping God made himself [580] and worked with his own hands as a favor to Zeus his father. On it was much curious work, wonderful to see; for of the many creatures which the land and sea rear up, he put most upon it, wonderful things, like living beings with voices: and great beauty shone out from it.

1 A Scholiast explains: "Either because they (men) sprang from the Melian nymphs (cp. 1. 187) ; or because, when they were born (?) , they cast themselves under the ash-trees (μέλιαι) , that is, the trees." The reference may be to the origin of men from ash-trees: cp. Works and Days, 145 and note.

Lines 585-616

But when he had made the beautiful evil to be the price for the blessing, he brought her out, delighting in the finery which the bright-eyed daughter of a mighty father had given her, to the place where the other gods and men were. And wonder took hold of the deathless gods and mortal men when they saw that which was sheer guile, not to be withstood by men. [590] For from her is the race of women and female kind: of her is the deadly race and tribe of women who live amongst mortal men to their great trouble, no helpmeets in hateful poverty, but only in wealth. And as in thatched hives bees [595] feed the drones whose nature is to do mischief—by day and throughout the day until the sun goes down the bees are busy and lay the white combs, while the drones stay at home in the covered hives and reap the toil of others into their own bellies— [600] even so Zeus who thunders on high made women to be an evil to mortal men, with a nature to do evil. And he gave them a second evil to be the price for the good they had: whoever avoids marriage and the sorrows that women cause, and will not wed, reaches deadly old age [605] without anyone to tend his years, and though he at least has no lack of livelihood while he lives, yet, when he is dead, his kinsfolk divide his possessions amongst them. And as for the man who chooses the lot of marriage and takes a good wife suited to his mind, evil continually contends with good; [610] for whoever happens to have mischievous children, lives always with unceasing grief in his spirit and heart within him; and this evil cannot be healed. So it is not possible to deceive or go beyond the will of Zeus: for not even the son of Iapetus, kindly Prometheus, [615] escaped his heavy anger, but of necessity strong bands confined him, although he knew many a wile.

Lines 617-653

But when first their father was vexed in his heart with Obriareus and Cottus and Gyes, he bound them in cruel bonds, because he was jealous of their exceeding manhood and comeliness [620] and great size: and he made them live beneath the wide-pathed earth, where they were afflicted, being set to dwell under the ground, at the end of the earth, at its great borders, in bitter anguish for a long time and with great grief at heart. But the son of Cronos and the other deathless gods [625] whom rich-haired Rhea bore from union with Cronos, brought them up again to the light at Earth's advising. For she herself recounted all things to the gods fully, how with these they might gain victory and a glorious cause to vaunt themselves. [630] For the Titan gods and as many as sprang from Cronos had long been fighting together in stubborn war with heart-grieving toil, the lordly Titans from high Othrys, but the gods, givers of good, whom rich-haired Rhea bore in union with Cronos, from Olympus. [635] So they, with bitter wrath, were fighting continually with one another at that time for ten full years, and the hard strife had no close or end for either side, and the issue of the war hung evenly balanced. But when he had provided those three with all things fitting, [640] nectar and ambrosia which the gods themselves eat, and when their proud spirit revived within them all after they had fed on nectar and delicious ambrosia, then it was that the father of men and gods spoke amongst them: "Hear me, bright children of Earth and Heaven, [645] that I may say what my heart within me bids. A long while now have we, who are sprung from Cronos and the Titan gods, fought with each other every day to get victory and to prevail. But show your great might and unconquerable strength, and [650] face the Titans in bitter strife; for remember our friendly kindness, and from what sufferings you are come back to the light from your cruel bondage under misty gloom through our counsels."

Lines 654-686

So he said. And blameless Cottus answered him again: " [655] Divine one, you speak that which we know well: no, even of ourselves we know that your wisdom and understanding is exceeding, and that you became a defender of the deathless ones from chill doom. And through your devising we have come back again from the murky gloom and from our merciless bonds, [660] enjoying what we looked not for, O lord, son of Cronos. And so now with fixed purpose and deliberate counsel we will aid your power in dreadful strife and will fight against the Titans in hard battle." So he said: and the gods, givers of good things, applauded when [665] they heard his word, and their spirit longed for war even more than before, and they all, both male and female, stirred up hated battle that day, the Titan gods, and all that were born of Cronos together with those dread, mighty ones of overwhelming strength [670] whom Zeus brought up to the light from Erebus beneath the earth. A hundred arms sprang from the shoulders of all alike, and each had fifty heads growing from his shoulders upon stout limbs. These, then, stood against the Titans in grim strife, [675] holding huge rocks in their strong hands. And on the other part the Titans eagerly strengthened their ranks, and both sides at one time showed the work of their hands and their might. The boundless sea rang terribly around, and the earth crashed loudly: wide Heaven was shaken and [680] groaned, and high Olympus reeled from its foundation under the charge of the undying gods, and a heavy quaking reached dim Tartarus and the deep sound of their feet in the fearful onset and of their hard missiles. So, then, they launched their grievous shafts upon one another, [685] and the cry of both armies as they shouted reached to starry heaven; and they met together with a great battle-cry.

Lines 687-728

Then Zeus no longer held back his might; but straight his heart was filled with fury and he showed forth all his strength. From Heaven and from Olympus [690] he came immediately, hurling his lightning: the bolts flew thick and fast from his strong hand together with thunder and lightning, whirling an awesome flame. The life-giving earth crashed around in burning, and the vast wood crackled loud with fire all about. [695] All the land seethed, and Ocean's streams and the unfruitful sea. The hot vapor lapped round the earthborn Titans: flame unspeakable rose to the bright upper air: the flashing glare of the thunderstone and lightning blinded their eyes for all that they were strong. [700] Astounding heat seized Chaos: and to see with eyes and to hear the sound with ears it seemed even as if Earth and wide Heaven above came together; for such a mighty crash would have arisen if Earth were being hurled to ruin, and Heaven from on high were hurling her down; [705] so great a crash was there while the gods were meeting together in strife. Also the winds brought rumbling earthquake and duststorm, thunder and lightning and the lurid thunderbolt, which are the shafts of great Zeus, and carried the clangor and the warcry into the midst of the two hosts. A horrible uproar [710] of terrible strife arose: mighty deeds were shown and the battle inclined. But until then, they kept at one another and fought continually in cruel war. And amongst the foremost Cottus and Briareos and Gyes insatiate for war [715] raised fierce fighting: three hundred rocks, one upon another, they launched from their strong hands and overshadowed the Titans with their missiles, and hurled them beneath the wide-pathed earth, and bound them in bitter chains when they had conquered them by their strength for all their great spirit, [720] as far beneath the earth as heaven is above earth; for so far is it from earth to Tartarus. For a brazen anvil falling down from heaven nine nights and days would reach the earth upon the tenth: and again, a brazen anvil falling from earth nine nights and days [725] would reach Tartarus upon the tenth. Round it runs a fence of bronze, and night spreads in triple line all about it like a neck-circlet, while above grow the roots of the earth and unfruitful sea.

Lines 729-766

There by the counsel of Zeus who drives the clouds the Titan gods [730] are hidden under misty gloom, in a dank place where are the ends of the huge earth. And they may not go out; for Poseidon fixed gates of bronze upon it, and a wall runs all round it on every side. There Gyes and Cottus and great-souled Obriareus [735] live, trusty warders of Zeus who holds the aegis. And there, all in their order, are the sources and ends of gloomy earth and misty Tartarus and the unfruitful sea and starry heaven, loathsome and dank, which even the gods abhor. [740] It is a great gulf, and if once a man were within the gates, he would not reach the floor until a whole year had reached its end, but cruel blast upon blast would carry him this way and that. And this marvel is awful even to the deathless gods. There stands the awful home of murky Night [745] wrapped in dark clouds. In front of it the son of Iapetus[1] stands immovably upholding the wide heaven upon his head and unwearying hands, where Night and Day draw near and greet one another as they pass the great threshold [750] of bronze: and while the one is about to go down into the house, the other comes out at the door. And the house never holds them both within; but always one is without the house passing over the earth, while the other stays at home and waits until the time for her journeying comes; [755] and the one holds all-seeing light for them on earth, but the other holds in her arms Sleep the brother of Death, even evil Night, wrapped in a vaporous cloud. And there the children of dark Night have their dwellings, Sleep and Death, awful gods. [760] The glowing Sun never looks upon them with his beams, neither as he goes up into heaven, nor as he comes down from heaven. And the former of them roams peacefully over the earth and the sea's broad back and is kindly to men; but the other has a heart of iron, and his spirit within him [765] is pitiless as bronze: whomever of men he has once seized he holds fast: and he is hateful even to the deathless gods.

1 Sc.Atlas, the Shu of Egyptian mythology: cp. note on line 177.

Lines 767-806

There, in front, stand the echoing halls of the god of the lower-world, strong Hades, and of awful Persephone. A fearful hound guards the house in front, [770] pitiless, and he has a cruel trick. On those who go in he fawns with his tail and both his ears, but suffers them not to go out back again, but keeps watch and devours whomever he catches going out of the gates of strong Hades and awful Persephone. [775] And there dwells the goddess loathed by the deathless gods, terrible Styx, eldest daughter of backflowing[1]Ocean. She lives apart from the gods in her glorious house vaulted over with great rocks and propped up to heaven all round with silver pillars. [780] Rarely does the daughter of Thaumas, swift-footed Iris, come to her with a message over the sea's wide back. But when strife and quarrel arise among the deathless gods, and when any one of them who live in the house of Olympus lies, then Zeus sends Iris to bring in a golden jug the great oath of the gods [785] from far away, the famous cold water which trickles down from a high and beetling rock. Far under the wide-pathed earth a branch of Oceanus flows through the dark night out of the holy stream, and a tenth part of his water is allotted to her. [790] With nine silver-swirling streams he winds about the earth and the sea's wide back, and then falls into the main[2]; but the tenth flows out from a rock, a sore trouble to the gods. For whoever of the deathless gods that hold the peaks of snowy Olympus pours a libation of her water and is forsworn, [795] must lie breathless until a full year is completed, and never come near to taste ambrosia and nectar, but lie spiritless and voiceless on a strewn bed: and a heavy trance overshadows him. But when he has spent a long year in his sickness, [800] another penance more hard follows after the first. For nine years he is cut off from the eternal gods and never joins their councils or their feasts, nine full years. But in the tenth year he comes again to join the assemblies of the deathless gods who live in the house of Olympus. [805] Such an oath, then, did the gods appoint the eternal and primeval water of Styx to be: and it spouts through a rugged place.

1 Oceanus is here regarded as a continuous stream enclosing the earth and the seas, and so as flowing back upon himself.

2 The conception of Oceanus is here different: he has nine streams which encircle the earth and the flow out into the "main" which appears to be the waste of waters on which, according to early Greek and Hebrew cosmology, the disk-like earth floated.

Lines 807-819

And there, all in their order, are the sources and ends of the dark earth and misty Tartarus and the unfruitful sea and starry heaven, [810] loathsome and dank, which even the gods abhor. And there are shining gates and an immovable threshold of bronze having unending roots, and it is grown of itself.[1] And beyond, away from all the gods, live the Titans, beyond gloomy Chaos. [815] But the glorious allies of loud-crashing Zeus have their dwelling upon Ocean's foundations, even Cottus and Gyes; but Briareos, being goodly, the deep-roaring Earth-Shaker made his son-in-law, giving him Cymopolea his daughter to wed.

1 I.e. the threshold is of "native" metal, and not artificial.

Lines 820-852

But when Zeus had driven the Titans from heaven, huge Earth bore her youngest child Typhoeus of the love of Tartarus, by the aid of golden Aphrodite. Strength was with his hands in all that he did and the feet of the strong god were untiring. From his shoulders [825] grew a hundred heads of a snake, a fearful dragon, with dark, flickering tongues, and from under the brows of his eyes in his marvellous heads flashed fire, and fire burned from his heads as he glared. And there were voices in all his dreadful heads [830] which uttered every kind of sound unspeakable; for at one time they made sounds such that the gods understood, but at another, the noise of a bull bellowing aloud in proud ungovernable fury; and at another, the sound of a lion, relentless of heart; and at another, sounds like whelps, wonderful to hear; [835] and again, at another, he would hiss, so that the high mountains re-echoed. And truly a thing past help would have happened on that day, and he would have come to reign over mortals and immortals, had not the father of men and gods been quick to perceive it. But he thundered hard and mightily: and the earth around [840] resounded terribly and the wide heaven above, and the sea and Ocean's streams and the nether parts of the earth. Great Olympus reeled beneath the divine feet of the king as he arose and earth groaned thereat. And through the two of them heat took hold on the dark-blue sea, [845] through the thunder and lightning, and through the fire from the monster, and the scorching winds and blazing thunderbolt. The whole earth seethed, and sky and sea: and the long waves raged along the beaches round and about at the rush of the deathless gods: and there arose an endless shaking. [850] Hades trembled where he rules over the dead below, and the Titans under Tartarus who live with Cronos, because of the unending clamor and the fearful strife.

Lines 853-885

So when Zeus had raised up his might and seized his arms, thunder and lightning and lurid thunderbolt, [855] he leaped from Olympus and struck him, and burned all the marvellous heads of the monster about him. But when Zeus had conquered him and lashed him with strokes, Typhoeus was hurled down, a maimed wreck, so that the huge earth groaned. And flame shot forth from the thunderstricken lord [860] in the dim rugged glens of the mount,[1]when he was smitten. A great part of huge earth was scorched by the terrible vapor and melted as tin melts when heated by men's art in channelled[2]crucibles; or as iron, which is hardest of all things, is shortened [865] by glowing fire in mountain glens and melts in the divine earth through the strength of Hephaestus.[3]Even so, then, the earth melted in the glow of the blazing fire. And in the bitterness of his anger Zeus cast him into wide Tartarus. And from Typhoeus come boisterous winds which blow damply, [870] except Notus and Boreas and clear Zephyr. These are a god-sent kind, and a great blessing to men; but the others blow fitfully upon the sea. Some rush upon the misty sea and work great havoc among men with their evil, raging blasts; [875] for varying with the season they blow, scattering ships and destroying sailors. And men who meet these upon the sea have no help against the mischief. Others again over the boundless, flowering earth spoil the fair fields of men who dwell below, [880] filling them with dust and cruel uproar. But when the blessed gods had finished their toil, and settled by force their struggle for honors with the Titans, they pressed far-seeing Olympian Zeus to reign and to rule over them, by Earth's prompting. So he divided their dignities amongst them.

1 According to Homer Typhoeus was overwhelmed by Zeus amongst the Arimi in Cilicia. Pindar represents him as buried under Aetna, and Tzetzes read Aetna in this passage.

2 The epithet (which means literally well-bored) seems to refer to the spout of the crucible.

3 The fire god. There is no reference to volcanic action: iron was smelted on Mount Ida; cp.Epigrams of Homer,ix. 2-4.

Lines 886-900

Now Zeus, king of the gods, made Metis his wife first, and she was wisest among gods and mortal men. But when she was about to bring forth the goddess bright-eyed Athena, Zeus craftily deceived her [890] with cunning words and put her in his own belly, as Earth and starry Heaven advised. For they advised him so, to the end that no other should hold royal sway over the eternal gods in place of Zeus; for very wise children were destined to be born of her, [895] first the maiden bright-eyed Tritogeneia, equal to her father in strength and in wise understanding; but afterwards she was to bear a son of overbearing spirit king of gods and men. But Zeus put her into his own belly first, [900] that the goddess might devise for him both good and evil.

Lines 901-937

Next he married bright Themis who bore the Horae (Hours) , and Eunomia (Order) ,

Dikë (Justice), and blooming Eirene (Peace), who mind the works of mortal men, and the Moerae (Fates) to whom wise Zeus gave the greatest honor, [905] Clotho, and Lachesis, and Atropos who give mortal men evil and good to have. And Eurynome, the daughter of Ocean, beautiful in form, bore him three fair-cheeked Charites (Graces), Aglaea, and Euphrosyne, and lovely Thaleia, [910] from whose eyes as they glanced flowed love that unnerves the limbs: and beautiful is their glance beneath their brows. Also he came to the bed of all-nourishing Demeter, and she bore white-armed Persephone whom Aidoneus carried off from her mother; but wise Zeus gave her to him. [915] And again, he loved Mnemosyne with the beautiful hair: and of her the nine gold-crowned Muses were born who delight in feasts and the pleasures of song. And Leto was joined in love with Zeus who holds the aegis, [920] and bore Apollo and Artemis delighting in arrows, children lovely above all the sons of Heaven. Lastly, he made Hera his blooming wife: and she was joined in love with the king of gods and men, and brought forth Hebe and Ares and Eileithyia. But Zeus himself gave birth from his own head to bright-eyed Tritogeneia,[1] [925] the awful, the strife-stirring, the host-leader, the unwearying, the queen, who delights in tumults and wars and battles. But Hera without union with Zeus—for she was very angry and quarrelled with her mate—bare famous Hephaestus, who is skilled in crafts more than all the sons of Heaven. [929a] But Hera was very angry and quarrelled with her mate. And because of this strife she bore without union with Zeus who holds the aegis a glorious son, Hephaestus, who excelled all the sons of Heaven in crafts. [929e] But Zeus lay with the fair-cheeked daughter of Ocean and Tethys apart from Hera . . . deceiving Metis (Thought) although she was full wise. But he seized her with his hands and put her in his belly, for fear that she might bring forth something stronger than his thunderbolt: [929j] therefore did Zeus, who sits on high and dwells in the aether, swallow her down suddenly. But she straightway conceived Pallas Athena: and the father of men and gods gave her birth by way of his head on the banks of the river Trito. And she remained hidden beneath the inward parts of Zeus, [929o] even Metis, Athena's mother, worker of righteousness, who was wiser than gods and mortal men. There the goddess (Athena) received that[2]whereby she excelled in strength all the deathless less ones who dwell in Olympus, she who made the host-scaring weapon of Athena. [929t] And with it (Zeus) gave her birth, arrayed in arms of war. [930] And of Amphitrite and the loud-roaring Earth-Shaker was born great, wide-ruling Triton, and he owns the depths of the sea, living with his dear mother and the lord his father in their golden house, an awful god. Also Cytherea bore to Ares the shield-piercer Panic and Fear, [935] terrible gods who drive in disorder the close ranks of men in numbing war, with the help of Ares, sacker of towns; and Harmonia whom high-spirited Cadmus made his wife.

1 I.e. Athena, who was born "on the banks of the river Trito" (cp. l. 929l).

2 Sc. the aegis. Line 929s is probably spurious, since it disagrees with 929q and contains a suspicious reference to Athens.

And Maia, the daughter of Atlas, bore to Zeus glorious Hermes, the herald of the deathless gods, for she went up into his holy bed. [940] And Semele, daughter of Cadmus was joined with him in love and bore him a splendid son, joyous Dionysus,—a mortal woman an immortal son. And now they both are gods. And Alcmena was joined in love with Zeus who drives the clouds and bore mighty Heracles. [945] And Hephaestus, the famous Lame One, made Aglaea, youngest of the Graces, his buxom wife. And golden-haired Dionysus made brown-haired Ariadne, the daughter of Minos, his buxom wife: and the son of Cronos made her deathless and unageing for him. [950] And mighty Heracles, the valiant son of neat-ankled Alcmena, when he had finished his grievous toils, made Hebe the child of great Zeus and goldshod Hera his shy wife in snowy Olympus. Happy he! For he has finished his great work [955] and lives amongst the undying gods, untroubled and unaging all his days. And Perseis, the daughter of Ocean, bore to unwearying Helios Circe and Aeetes the king. And Aeetes, the son of Helios who shows light to men, [960] took to wife fair-cheeked Idyia, daughter of Ocean the perfect stream, by the will of the gods: and she was subject to him in love through golden Aphrodite and bore him neat-ankled Medea.

And now farewell, you dwellers on Olympus, and you islands and continents, and you briny sea within. [965] Now sing the company of goddesses, sweet-voiced Muses of Olympus, daughter of Zeus who holds the aegis,—even those deathless ones who lay with mortal men and bore children like gods. Demeter, bright goddess, was joined in sweet love [970] with the hero Iasion in a thrice-ploughed fallow in the rich land of Crete, and bore Plutus, a kindly god who goes everywhere over land and the sea's wide back, and he makes rich the man who finds him and into whose hands he comes, bestowing great wealth upon him. [975] And Harmonia, the daughter of golden Aphrodite, bore to Cadmus Ino and Semele and fair-cheeked Agave and Autonoe whom long haired Aristaeus wedded, and Polydorus also in rich-crowned Thebes. And the daughter of Ocean, Callirrhoe [980] was joined in the love of rich Aphrodite with stout-hearted Chrysaor and bore a son who was the strongest of all men, Geryones, whom mighty Heracles killed in sea-girt Erythea for the sake of his shambling oxen. And Eos bore to Tithonus brazen-crested Memnon, [985] king of the Ethiopians, and the Lord Emathion. And to Cephalus she bore a splendid son, strong Phaethon, a man like the gods, whom, when he was a young boy in the tender flower of glorious youth with childish thoughts, laughter-loving Aphrodite [990] seized and caught up and made a keeper of her shrine by night, a divine spirit. And the son of Aeson by the will of the gods led away from Aeetes the daughter of Aeetes the heaven-nurtured king, when he had finished the many grievous labours [995] which the great king, overbearing Pelias, that outrageous and presumptuous doer of violence, put upon him. But when the son of Aeson had finished them, he came to Iolcus after long toil bringing the coy-eyed girl with him on his swift ship, and made her his buxom wife. [1000] And she was subject to Iason, shepherd of the people, and bore a son Medeus whom Cheiron the son of Philyra brought up in the mountains. And the will of great Zeus was fulfilled.

Lines 1003-End

But of the daughters of Nereus, the Old man of the Sea, Psamathe the fair goddess, [1005] was loved by Aeacus through golden Aphrodite and bore Phocus. And the silver-shod goddess Thetis was subject to Peleus and brought forth lion-hearted Achilles, the destroyer of men. And Cytherea with the beautiful crown was joined in sweet love with the hero Anchises and bore Aeneas [1010] on the peaks of Ida with its many wooded glens. And Circe the daughter of Helius, Hyperion's son, loved steadfast Odysseus and bore Agrius and Latinus who was faultless and strong: also she brought forth Telegonus by the will of golden Aphrodite. [1015] And they ruled over the famous Tyrsenians, very far off in a recess of the holy islands. And the bright goddess Calypso was joined to Odysseus in sweet love, and bore him Nausithous and Nausinous. [1020] These are the immortal goddesses who lay with mortal men and bore them children like gods. But now, sweet-voiced Muses of Olympus, daughters of Zeus who holds the aegis, sing of the company of women.

Works & Days

Lines 1-10

Muses of Pieria who give glory through song, come hither, tell of Zeus your father and chant his praise. Through him mortal men are famed or unfamed, sung or unsung alike, as great Zeus wills. [5] For easily he makes strong, and easily he brings the strong man low; easily he humbles the proud and raises the obscure, and easily he straightens the crooked and blasts the proud,— Zeus who thunders aloft and has his dwelling most high. Attend thou with eye and ear, and make judgements straight with righteousness. [10] And, Perses, I would tell of true things.

Lines 11-41

So, after all, there was not one kind of Strife alone, but all over the earth there are two. As for the one, a man would praise her when he came to understand her; but the other is blameworthy: and they are wholly different in nature. For one fosters evil war and battle, being cruel: [15] her no man loves; but perforce, through the will of the deathless gods, men pay harsh Strife her honor due. But the other is the elder daughter of dark Night, and the son of Cronos who sits above and dwells in the aether, set her in the roots of the earth: and she is far kinder to men. [20] She stirs up even the shiftless to toil; for a man grows eager to work when he considers his neighbor, a rich man who hastens to plough and plant and put his house in good order; and neighbor vies with his neighbor as he hurries after wealth. This Strife is wholesome for men. [25] And potter is angry with potter, and craftsman with craftsman, and beggar is jealous of beggar, and minstrel of minstrel. Perses, lay up these things in your heart, and do not let that Strife who delights in mischief hold your heart back from work, while you peep and peer and listen to the wrangles of the court-house. [30] Little concern has he with quarrels and courts who has not a year's victuals laid up betimes, even that which the earth bears, Demeter's grain. When you have got plenty of that, you can raise disputes and strive to get another's goods. But you shall have no second chance [35] to deal so again: nay, let us settle our dispute here with true judgement which is of Zeus and is perfect. For we had already divided our inheritance, but you seized the greater share and carried it off, greatly swelling the glory of our bribe-swallowing lords who love to judge such a cause as this. [40] Fools! They know not how much more the half is than the whole, nor what great advantage there is in mallow and asphodel.[1]

1 That is, the poor man's fare, like "bread and cheese."

Lines 42-58

For the gods keep hidden from men the means of life. Else you would easily do work enough in a day to supply you for a full year even without working; [45] soon would you put away your rudder over the smoke, and the fields worked by ox and sturdy mule would run to waste. But Zeus in the anger of his heart hid it, because Prometheus the crafty deceived him; therefore he planned sorrow and mischief against men. [50] He hid fire; but that the noble son of Iapetus stole again for men from Zeus the counsellor in a hollow fennel-stalk, so that Zeus who delights in thunder did not see it. But afterwards Zeus who gathers the clouds said to him in anger: "Son of Iapetus, surpassing all in cunning, [55] you are glad that you have outwitted me and stolen fire— a great plague to you yourself and to men that shall be. But I will give men as the price for fire an evil thing in which they may all be glad of heart while they embrace their own destruction."

Lines 59-82

So said the father of men and gods, and laughed aloud. [60] And he bade famous Hephaestus make haste and mix earth with water and to put in it the voice and strength of human kind, and fashion a sweet, lovely maiden-shape, like to the immortal goddesses in face; and Athena to teach her needlework and the weaving of the varied web; [65] and golden Aphrodite to shed grace upon her head and cruel longing and cares that weary the limbs. And he charged Hermes the guide, the Slayer of Argus, to put in her a shameless mind and a deceitful nature. So he ordered. And they obeyed the lord Zeus the son of Cronos. [70] Forthwith the famous Lame God moulded clay in the likeness of a modest maid, as the son of Cronos purposed. And the goddess brighteyed Athena girded and clothed her, and the divine Graces and queenly Persuasion put necklaces of gold upon her, [75] and the rich-haired Hours crowned her head with spring flowers. And Pallas Athena bedecked her form with all manner of finery. Also the Guide, the Slayer of Argus, contrived within her lies and crafty words and a deceitful nature at the will of loud thundering Zeus, [80] and the Herald of the gods put speech in her. And he called this woman Pandora,[1] because all they who dwelt on Olympus gave each a gift, a plague to men who eat bread.

1 The All-endowed.

Lines 83-108

But when he had finished the sheer, hopeless snare, the Father sent glorious Argus-Slayer, [85] the swift messenger of the gods, to take it to Epimetheus as a gift. And Epimetheus did not think on what Prometheus had said to him, bidding him never take a gift of Olympian Zeus, but to send it back for fear it might prove to be something harmful to men. But he took the gift, and afterwards, when the evil thing was already his, he understood. [90] For ere this the tribes of men lived on earth remote and free from ills and hard toil and heavy sicknesses which bring the Fates upon men; for in misery men grow old quickly. But the woman took off the great lid of the jar[1] with her hands [95] and scattered, all these and her thought caused sorrow and mischief to men. Only Hope remained there in an unbreakable home within under the rim of the great jar, and did not fly out at the door; for ere that, the lid of the jar stopped her, by the will of Aegis-holding Zeus who gathers the clouds. [100] But the rest, countless plagues, wander amongst men; for earth is full of evils, and the sea is full. Of themselves diseases come upon men continually by day and by night, bringing mischief to mortals silently; for wise Zeus took away speech from them. [105] So is there no way to escape the will of Zeus. Or if you will, I will sum you up another tale well and skilfully—and do you lay it up in your heart,—how the gods and mortal men sprang from one source.

1 The jar or casket contained the gifts of the gods mentioned in 1. 82.

Lines 109-139

First of all [110] the deathless gods who dwell on Olympus made a golden race of mortal men who lived in the time of Cronos when he was reigning in heaven. And they lived like gods [115] without sorrow of heart, remote and free from toil and grief: miserable age rested not on them; but with legs and arms never failing they made merry with feasting beyond the reach of all evils. When they died, it was as though they were overcome with sleep, and they had all good things; for the fruitful earth unforced bare them fruit abundantly and without stint. They dwelt in ease and peace upon their lands with many good things, [120] rich in flocks and loved by the blessed gods. But after the earth had covered this generation—they are called pure spirits dwelling on the earth, and are kindly, delivering from harm, and guardians of mortal men; [125] for they roam everywhere over the earth, clothed in mist and keep watch on judgements and cruel deeds, givers of wealth; for this royal right also they received;—then they who dwell on Olympus made a second generation which was of silver and less noble by far. It was like the golden race neither in body nor in spirit. [130] A child was brought up at his good mother's side a hundred years, an utter simpleton, playing childishly in his own home. But when they were full grown and were come to the full measure of their prime, they lived only a little time and that in sorrow because of their foolishness, for they could not keep from sinning and [135] from wronging one another, nor would they serve the immortals, nor sacrifice on the holy altars of the blessed ones as it is right for men to do wherever they dwell. Then Zeus the son of Cronos was angry and put them away, because they would not give honor to the blessed gods who live on Olympus.

Lines 140-173

But when earth had covered this generation also—they are called blessed spirits of the underworld by men, and, though they are of second order, yet honor attends them also—Zeus the Father made a third generation of mortal men, a brazen race, sprung from ash-trees[1] ; and it was in no way equal to the silver age, [145] but was terrible and strong. They loved the lamentable works of Ares and deeds of violence; they ate no bread, but were hard of heart like adamant, fearful men. Great was their strength and unconquerable the arms which grew from their shoulders on their strong limbs. [150] Their armor was of bronze, and their houses of bronze, and of bronze were their implements: there was no black iron. These were destroyed by their own hands and passed to the dank house of chill Hades, and left no name: terrible though they were, [155] black Death seized them, and they left the bright light of the sun. But when earth had covered this generation also, Zeus the son of Cronos made yet another, the fourth, upon the fruitful earth, which was nobler and more righteous, a god-like race of hero-men who are called [160] demi-gods, the race before our own, throughout the boundless earth. Grim war and dread battle destroyed a part of them, some in the land of Cadmus at seven-gated Thebes when they fought for the flocks of Oedipus, and some, when it had brought them in ships over the great sea gulf [165] to Troy for rich-haired Helen's sake: there death's end enshrouded a part of them. But to the others father Zeus the son of Cronos gave a living and an abode apart from men, and made them dwell at the ends of earth. [170] And they live untouched by sorrow in the islands of the blessed along the shore of deep-swirling Ocean, happy heroes for whom [173] the grain-giving earth bears honey-sweet fruit flourishing thrice a year, [169] far from the deathless gods, and Cronos rules over them; [169a] for the father of men and gods released him from his bonds. [169b] And these last equally have honor and glory. [169c] And again far-seeing Zeus made yet another generation, the fifth, of men [169d] who are upon the bounteous earth.

1 Eustathius refers to Hesiod as stating that men sprung "from oaks and stones and ashtrees."Proclus believed that the Nymphs called Meliae (*Theogony,*187) are intended. Goettling would render: "A race terrible because of their (ashen) spears."

Lines 174-201

Thereafter, would that I were not among the men of the fifth generation, [175] but either had died before or been born afterwards. For now truly is a race of iron, and men never rest from labor and sorrow by day, and from perishing by night; and the gods shall lay sore trouble upon them. But, notwithstanding, even these shall have some good mingled with their evils. [180] And Zeus will destroy this race of mortal men also when they come to have grey hair on the temples at their birth.[1] The father will not agree with his children, nor the children with their father, nor guest with his host, nor comrade with comrade; nor will brother be dear to brother as aforetime. [185] Men will dishonor their parents as they grow quickly old, and will carp at them, chiding them with bitter words, hard-hearted they, not knowing the fear of the gods. They will not repay their aged parents the cost of their nurture, for might shall be their right: and one man will sack another's city. [190] There will be no favor for the man who keeps his oath or for the just or for the good; but rather men will praise the evil-doer and his violent dealing. Strength will be right, and reverence will cease to be; and the wicked will hurt the worthy man, speaking false words against him, and will swear an oath upon them. [195] Envy, foul-mouthed, delighting in evil, with scowling face, will go along with wretched men one and all. [200] And then Aidos and Nemesis,[2] with their sweet forms wrapped in white robes, will go from the wide-pathed earth and forsake mankind to join the company of the deathless gods: and bitter sorrows will be left for mortal men, and there will be no help against evil.

1 *I.e.*the race will so degenerate that at the last even a new-born child will show the marks of old age.

2 Aidos, as a quality, is that feeling of reverence or shame which restrains men from wrong; Nemesis is the feeling of righteous indignation aroused especially by the sight of the wicked in undeserved prosperity (*cf. Psalms,*lxxii. 1-19) .

Lines 202-237

And now I will tell a fable for princes who themselves understand. Thus said the hawk to the nightingale with speckled neck, while he carried her high up among the clouds, gripped fast in his talons, [205] and she, pierced by his crooked talons, cried pitifully. To her he spoke disdainfully: "Miserable thing, why do you cry out? One far stronger than you now holds you fast, and you must go wherever I take you, songstress as you are. And if I please, I will make my meal of you, or let you go. [210] He is a fool who tries to withstand the stronger, for he does not get the mastery and suffers pain besides his shame." So said the swiftly flying hawk, the long-winged bird. But you, Perses, listen to right and do not foster violence; for violence is bad for a poor man. [215] Even the prosperous cannot easily bear its burden, but is weighed down under it when he has fallen into delusion. The better path is to go by on the other side towards Justice; for Justice beats Outrage when she comes at length to the end of the race. But only when he has suffered does the fool learn this. For Oath keeps pace with wrong judgements. [220] There is a noise when Justice is being dragged in the way where those who devour bribes and give sentence with crooked judgements, take her. And she, wrapped in mist, follows to the city and haunts of the people, weeping, and bringing mischief to men, even to such as have driven her forth in that they did not deal straightly with her. [225] But they who give straight judgements to strangers and to the men of the land, and go not aside from what is just, their city flourishes, and the people prosper in it: Peace, the nurse of children, is abroad in their land, and all-seeing Zeus never decrees cruel war against them. [230] Neither famine nor disaster ever haunt men who do true justice; but light-heartedly they tend the fields which are all their care. The earth bears them victual in plenty, and on the mountains the oak bears acorns upon the top and bees in the midst. Their woolly sheep are laden with fleeces; [235] their women bear children like their parents. They flourish continually with good things, and do not travel on ships, for the grain-giving earth bears them fruit.

Lines 238-273

But for those who practice violence and cruel deeds far-seeing Zeus, the son of Cronos, ordains a punishment. [240] Often even a whole city suffers for a bad man who sins and devises presumptuous deeds, and the son of Cronos lays great trouble upon the people, famine and plague together, so that the men perish away, and their women do not bear children, and their houses become few, [245] through the contriving of Olympian Zeus. And again, at another time, the son of Cronos either destroys their wide army, or their walls, or else makes an end of their ships on the sea. You princes, mark well this punishment, you also, for the deathless gods are near among men; and [250] mark all those who oppress their fellows with crooked judgements, and heed not the anger of the gods. For upon the bounteous earth Zeus has thrice ten thousand spirits, watchers of mortal men, and these keep watch on judgements and deeds of wrong [255] as they roam, clothed in mist, all over the earth. And there is virgin Justice, the daughter of Zeus, who is honored and reverenced among the gods who dwell on Olympus, and whenever anyone hurts her with lying slander, she sits beside her father, Zeus the son of Cronos, [260] and tells him of men's wicked heart, until the people pay for the mad folly of their princes who, evilly minded, pervert judgement and give sentence crookedly. Keep watch against this, you princes, and make straight your judgements, you who devour bribes; put crooked judgements altogether from your thoughts. [265] He does mischief to himself who does mischief to another, and evil planned harms the plotter most. The eye of Zeus, seeing all and understanding all, beholds these things too, if so he will, and fails not to mark what sort of justice is this that the city keeps within it. [270] Now, therefore, may neither I myself be righteous among men, nor my son—for then it is a bad thing to be righteous—if indeed the unrighteous shall have the greater right. But I think that all-wise Zeus will not yet bring that to pass.

Lines 274-319

But you, Perses, lay up these things within your heart and [275] listen now to right, ceasing altogether to think of violence. For the son of Cronos has ordained this law for men, that fishes and beasts and winged fowls should devour one another, for right is not in them; but to mankind he gave right which proves [280] far the best. For whoever knows the right and is ready to speak it, far-seeing Zeus gives him prosperity; but whoever deliberately lies in his witness and foreswears himself, and so hurts Justice and sins beyond repair, that man's generation is left obscure thereafter. [285] But the generation of the man who swears truly is better thenceforward. To you, foolish Perses, I will speak good sense. Badness can be got easily and in shoals; the road to her is smooth, and she lives very near us. But between us and Goodness the gods have placed the sweat of our brows; [290] long and steep is the path that leads to her, and it is rough at the first; but when a man has reached the top, then is she easy to reach, though before that she was hard. [295] That man is altogether best who considers all things himself and marks what will be better afterwards and at the end; and he, again, is good who listens to a good adviser; but whoever neither thinks for himself nor keeps in mind what another tells him, he is an unprofitable man. But do you at any rate, always remembering my charge, work, high-born Perses, that Hunger [300] may hate you, and venerable Demeter richly crowned may love you and fill your barn with food; for Hunger is altogether a meet comrade for the sluggard. Both gods and men are angry with a man who lives idle, [305] for in nature he is like the stingless drones who waste the labor of the bees, eating without working; but let it be your care to order your work properly, that in the right season your barns may be full of victual. Through work men grow rich in flocks and substance, and [309] working they are much better loved by the immortals.[1] [311] Work is no disgrace: it is idleness which is a disgrace. But if you work, the idle will soon envy you as you grow rich, for fame and renown attend on wealth. And whatever be your lot, work is best for you, [315] if you turn your misguided mind away from other men's property to your work and attend to your livelihood as I bid you. An evil shame is the needy man's companion, shame which both greatly harms and prospers men: shame is with poverty, but confidence with wealth.

Lines 320-369

Wealth should not be seized: god-given wealth is much better; for if a man takes great wealth violently and perforce, or if he steals it through his tongue, as often happens when gain deceives men's sense and dishonor tramples down honor, [325] the gods soon blot him out and make that man's house low, and wealth attends him only for a little time. Alike with him who does wrong to a suppliant or a guest, or who goes up to his brother's bed and commits unnatural sin in lying with his wife, [330] or who infatuately offends against fatherless children, or who abuses his old father at the cheerless threshold of old age and attacks him with harsh words, truly Zeus himself is angry, and at the last lays on him a heavy requital for his evil doing. [335] But do you turn your foolish heart altogether away from these things, and, as far as you are able, sacrifice to the deathless gods purely and cleanly, and burn rich meats also, and at other times propitiate them with libations and incense, both when you go to bed and when the holy light has come back, [340] that they may be gracious to you in heart and spirit, and so you may buy another's holding and not another yours. Call your friend to a feast; but leave your enemy alone; and especially call him who lives near you: for if any mischief happens in the place, [345] neighbors come ungirt, but kinsmen stay to gird themselves.[1] A bad neighbor is as great a plague as a good one is a great blessing; he who enjoys a good neighbor has a precious possession. Not even an ox would die but for a bad neighbor. Take fair measure from your neighbor and pay him back [350] fairly with the same measure, or better, if you can; so that if you are in need afterwards, you may find him sure. Do not get base gain: base gain is as bad as ruin. Be friends with the friendly, and visit him who visits you. Give to one who gives, but do not give to one who does not give. [355] A man gives to the free-handed, but no one gives to the closefisted. Give is a good girl, but Take is bad and she brings death. For the man who gives willingly, even though he gives a great thing, rejoices in his gift and is glad in heart; but whoever gives way to shamelessness and takes something himself, [360] even though it is a small thing, [363] it freezes his heart. He who adds to what he has, will keep off bright-eyed hunger; [361] for if you add only a little to a little and do this often, [362] soon that little will become great. What a man has by him at home does not trouble him: [365] it is better to have your stuff at home, for whatever is abroad may mean loss. It is a good thing to draw on what you have; but it grieves your heart to need something and not to have it, and I bid you mark this. Take your fill when the cask is first opened and when it is nearly spent, but midways be sparing: it is poor saving when you come to the lees.

1 *I.e.* neighbors come at once and without making preparations, but kinsmen by marriage (who live at a distance) have to prepare, and so are long in coming.

Lines 370-404

Let the wage promised to a friend be fixed; even with your brother smile—and get a witness; for trust and mistrust alike ruin men. Do not let a flaunting woman coax and cozen and deceive you: she is after your barn. The man who trusts womankind trusts deceivers. [375] There should be an only son to feed his father's house, for so wealth will increase in the home; but if you leave a second son you should die old. Yet Zeus can easily give great wealth to a greater number. [380] More hands mean more work and more increase. If your heart within you desires wealth, do these things and work with work upon work. When the Pleiades, daughters of Atlas, are rising,[1] begin your harvest, and your ploughing when they are going to set.[2] [385] Forty nights and days they are hidden and appear again as the year moves round, when first you sharpen your sickle. This is the law of the plains, and of those who live near the sea, [390] and who inhabit rich country, the glens and hollows far from the tossing sea,—strip to sow and strip to plough and strip to reap, if you wish to get in all Demeter's fruits in due season, and that each kind may grow in its season. Else, afterwards, you may chance to be in want, [395] and go begging to other men's houses, but without avail; as you have already come to me. But I will give you no more nor give you further measure. Foolish Perses! Work the work which the gods ordained for men, lest in bitter anguish of spirit you with your wife and children [400] seek your livelihood amongst your neighbors, and they do not heed you. Two or three times, may be, you will succeed, but if you trouble them further, it will not avail you, and all your talk will be in vain, and your word-play unprofitable. Nay, I bid you find a way to pay your debts and avoid hunger.

1 Early in May.

2 In November.

Lines 405-447

First of all, get a house, and a woman and an ox for the plough—a slave woman and not a wife, to follow the oxen as well—and make everything ready at home, so that you may not have to ask of another, and he refuse you, and so, because you are in lack, the season pass by and your work come to nothing. [410] Do not put your work off till to-morrow and the day after; for a sluggish worker does not fill his barn, nor one who puts off his work: industry makes work go well, but a man who puts off work is always at hand-grips with ruin. When the piercing power and sultry heat of the sun abate, [415] and almighty Zeus sends the autumn rains,[1] and men's flesh comes to feel far easier,—for then the star Sirius passes over the heads of men, who are born to misery, only a little while by day and takes greater share of night— [420] then, when it showers its leaves to the ground and stops sprouting, the wood you cut with your axe is least liable to worm. Then remember to hew your timber: it is the season for that work. Cut a mortar[2] three feet wide and a pestle three cubits long, and an axle of seven feet, for it will do very well so; [425] but if you make it eight feet long, you can cut a beetle[3] from it as well. Cut a felloe three spans across for a wagon of ten palms' width. Hew also many bent timbers, and bring home a plough-tree when you have found it, and look out on the mountain or in the field for one of holm-oak; [430] for this is the strongest for oxen to plough with when one of Athena's handmen has fixed in the share-beam and fastened it to the pole with dowels. Get two ploughs ready and work on them at home, one all of a piece, and the other jointed. It is far better to do this, for if you should break one of them, you can put the oxen to the other. [435] Poles of laurel or elm are most free from worms, and a share-beam of oak and a plough-tree of holm-oak. Get two oxen, bulls of nine years; for their strength is unspent and they are in the prime of their age: they are best for work. They will not fight in the furrow and break the plough [440] and then leave the work undone. Let a brisk fellow of forty years follow them, with a loaf of four quarters[4] and eight slices[5] for his dinner, one who will attend to his work and drive a straight furrow and is past the age for gaping after his fellows, [445] but will keep his mind on his work. No younger man will be better than he at scattering the seed and avoiding double-sowing; for a man less staid gets disturbed, hankering after his fellows.

1 In October.

2 For pounding corn.

3 A mallet for breaking clods after ploughing.

4 The loaf is a flattish cake with two intersecting lines scored on its upper surface which divide it into four equal parts.

5 The meaning is obscure. A scholiast renders "giving eight mouthfuls"; but the elder Philostratus uses the word in contrast to "leavened."

Lines 448-478

Mark, when you hear the voice of the crane[1] who cries year by year from the clouds above, [450] for she gives the signal for ploughing and shows the season of rainy winter; but she vexes the heart of the man who has no oxen. Then is the time to feed up your horned oxen in the byre; for it is easy to say: "Give me a yoke of oxen and a wagon," and it is easy to refuse: "I have work for my oxen." [455] The man who is rich in fancy thinks his wagon as good as built already—the fool! he does not know that there are a hundred timbers to a wagon. Take care to lay these up beforehand at home. So soon as the time for ploughing is proclaimed to men, then make haste, you and your slaves alike, [460] in wet and in dry, to plough in the season for ploughing, and bestir yourself early in the morning so that your fields may be full. Plough in the spring; but fallow broken up in the summer will not belie your hopes. Sow fallow land when the soil is still getting light: fallow land is a defender from harm and a soother of children. [465] Pray to Zeus of the Earth and to pure Demeter to make Demeter's holy grain sound and heavy, when first you begin ploughing, when you hold in your hand the end of the plough-tail and bring down your stick on the backs of the oxen as they draw on the pole-bar by the yoke-straps. [470] Let a slave follow a little behind with a mattock and make trouble for the birds by hiding the seed; for good management is the best for mortal men as bad management is the worst. In this way your corn-ears will bow to the ground with fullness if the Olympian himself gives a good result at the last, [475] and you will sweep the cobwebs from your bins and you will be glad, I think, as you take of your garnered substance. And so you will have plenty till you come to grey² springtime, and will not look wistfully to others, but another shall be in need of your help.

1 About the middle of November.

2 Spring is so described because the buds have not yet cast their iron-grey husks.

Lines 479-503

But if you plough the good ground at the solstice,¹ [480] you will reap sitting, grasping a thin crop in your hand, binding the sheaves awry, dust-covered, not glad at all; so you will bring all home in a basket and not many will admire you. Yet the will of Zeus who holds the aegis is different at different times; and it is hard for mortal men to tell it; [485] for if you should plough late, you may find this remedy—when the cuckoo first calls² in the leaves of the oak and makes men glad all over the boundless earth, if Zeus should send rain on the third day and not cease until it rises neither above an ox's hoof nor falls short of it, [490] then the late-plougher will vie with the early. Keep all this well in mind, and fail not to mark grey spring as it comes and the season of rain. Pass by the smithy and its crowded lounge in winter time when the cold keeps men from field work,— [495] for then an industrious man can greatly prosper his house—lest bitter winter catch you helpless and poor, and you chafe a swollen foot with a shrunk hand. [500] The idle man who waits on empty hope, lacking a livelihood, lays to heart mischief-making; it is not a wholesome hope that accompanies a needy man who lolls at ease while he has no sure livelihood.

1 In December.

2 In March.

Lines 504-535

While it is yet midsummer command your slaves: "It will not always be summer, build barns." Avoid the month Lenaeon,[1] wretched days, all of them fit to skin an ox, [505] and the frosts which are cruel when Boreas blows over the earth. He blows across horse-breeding Thrace upon the wide sea and stirs it up, while earth and the forest howl. On many a high-leafed oak and thick pine he falls [510] and brings them to the bounteous earth in mountain glens: then all the immense wood roars and the beasts shudder and put their tails between their legs, even those whose hide is covered with fur; for with his bitter blast he blows even through them, although they are shaggy-breasted. [515] He goes even through an ox's hide; it does not stop him. Also he blows through the goat's fine hair. But through the fleeces of sheep, because their wool is abundant, the keen wind Boreas pierces not at all; but it makes the old man curved as a wheel. And it does not blow through the tender maiden [520] who stays indoors with her dear mother, unlearned as yet in the works of golden Aphrodite, and who washes her soft body and anoints herself with oil and lies down in an inner room within the house, on a winter's day when the Boneless One[2] gnaws his foot [525] in his fireless house and wretched home; for the sun shows him no pastures to make for, but goes to and fro over the land and city of dusky men,[3] and shines more sluggishly upon the whole race of the Hellenes. Then the horned and unhorned denizens of the wood, [530] with teeth chattering pitifully, flee through the copses and glades, and all, as they seek shelter, have this one care, to gain thick coverts or some hollow rock. Then, like the Three-legged One[4] whose back is broken and whose head looks down upon the ground, [535] like him, I say, they wander to escape the white snow.

1 The latter part of January and earlier part of February.

2 *I.e.* the octopus or cuttle.

3 *I.e.* the dark-skinned people of Africa, the Egyptians or Aethiopians.

4 *I.e.* an old man walking with a staff (the "third leg"—as in the riddle of the Sphinx).

Lines 536-570

Then put on, as I bid you, a soft coat and a tunic to the feet to shield your body,—and you should weave thick woof on thin warp. In this clothe yourself so that your hair may keep still [540] and not bristle and stand upon end all over your body. Lace on your feet close-fitting boots of the hide of a slaughtered ox, thickly lined with felt inside. And when the season of frost comes on, stitch together skins of firstling kids with ox-sinew, to put over your back [545] and to keep off the rain. On your head above wear a shaped cap of felt to keep your ears from getting wet, for the dawn is chill when Boreas has once made his onslaught, and at dawn a fruitful mist is spread over the earth from starry heaven upon the fields of blessed men: [550] it is drawn from the ever-flowing rivers and is raised high above the earth by windstorm, and sometimes it turns to rain towards evening, and sometimes to wind when Thracian Boreas huddles the thick clouds. Finish your work and return home ahead of him, [555] and do not let the dark cloud from heaven wrap round you and make your body clammy and soak your clothes. Avoid it; for this is the hardest month, wintry, hard for sheep and hard for men. In this season let your oxen have half their usual food, but let your man have more; [560] for the helpful nights are long. Observe all this until the year is ended and you have nights and days of equal length, and Earth, the mother of all, bears again her various fruit. When Zeus has finished [565] sixty wintry days after the solstice, then the star Arcturus[1] leaves the holy stream of Ocean and first rises brilliant at dusk. After him the shrilly wailing daughter of Pandion, the swallow, appears to men when spring is just beginning. [570] Before she comes, prune the vines, for it is best so.

1 February to March.

Lines 571-608

But when the House-carrier[1] climbs up the plants from the earth to escape the Pleiades, then it is no longer the season for digging vineyards, but to whet your sickles and rouse up your slaves. Avoid shady seats and sleeping until dawn [575] in the harvest season, when the sun scorches the body. Then be busy and bring home your fruits, getting up early to make your livelihood sure. For dawn takes away a third part of your work, dawn advances a man on his journey and advances him in his work,— [580] dawn which appears and sets many men on their road, and puts yokes on many oxen. But when the artichoke flowers,[2] and the chirping grass-hopper sits in a tree and pours down his shrill song continually from under his wings in the season of wearisome heat, [585] then goats are plumpest and wine sweetest; women are most wanton, but men are feeblest, because Sirius parches head and knees and the skin is dry through heat. But at that time let me have a shady rock and wine of Biblis, [590] a clot of curds and milk of drained goats with the flesh of a heifer fed in the woods, that has never calved, and of firstling kids; then also let me drink bright wine, sitting in the shade, when my heart is satisfied with food, and so, turning my head to face the fresh Zephyr, [595] from the everflowing spring which pours down unfouled, thrice pour an offering of water, but make a fourth libation of wine. Set your slaves to winnow Demeter's holy grain, when strong Orion[3] first appears, on a smooth threshing-floor in an airy place. [600] Then measure it and store it in jars. And so soon as you have safely stored all your stuff indoors, I bid you put your bondman out of doors and seek out a servant-girl with no children;—for a servant with a child to nurse is troublesome. And look after the dog with jagged teeth; do not grudge him his food, [605] or some time the Day-sleeper[4] may take your stuff. Bring in fodder and litter so as to have enough for your oxen and mules. After that, let your men rest their poor knees and unyoke your pair of oxen.

1 *I.e.* the snail. The season is the middle of May.

2 In June.

3 July

4 *I.e.* a robber.

Lines 609-640

But when Orion and Sirius are come into midheaven, [610] and rosy-fingered Dawn sees Arcturus,[1] then cut off all the grape-clusters, Perses, and bring them home. Show them to the sun ten days and ten nights: then cover them over for five, and on the sixth day draw off into vessels the gifts of joyful Dionysus. But when [615] the Pleiades and Hyades and strong Orion begin to set,[2] then remember to plough in season: and so the completed year[3] will fitly pass beneath the earth.But if desire for uncomfortable sea-faring seize you when the Pleiades plunge into the misty sea[4] [620] to escape Orion's rude strength, then truly gales of all kinds rage. Then keep ships no longer on the sparkling sea, but be sure to till the land as I bid you. Haul up your ship upon the land and pack it closely with stones [625] all round to keep off the power of the winds which blow damply, and draw out the bilge-plug so that the rain of heaven may not rot it. Put away all the tackle and fittings in your house, and stow the wings of the sea-going ship neatly, and hang up the well-shaped rudder over the smoke. [630] You yourself wait until the season for sailing is come, and then haul your swift ship down to the sea and stow a convenient cargo in it, so that you may bring home profit, even as your father and mine, foolish Perses, used to sail on shipboard because he lacked sufficient livelihood. And one day he came to this very place, crossing over a great stretch of sea; [635] he left Aeolian Cyme and fled, not from riches and substance, but from wretched poverty which Zeus lays upon men, and he settled near Helicon in a miserable hamlet, [640] Ascra, which is bad in winter, sultry in summer, and good at no time.

1 September

2 The end of October.

3 That is, the succession of stars which make up the full year.

4 The end of October or beginning of November.

Lines 641-677

But you, Perses, remember all works in their season but sailing especially. Admire a small ship, but put your freight in a large one; for the greater the lading, the greater will be your piled gain, [645] if only the winds will keep back their harmful gales. If ever you turn your misguided heart to trading and wish to escape from debt and joyless hunger, I will show you the measures of the loud-roaring sea, though I have no skill in sea-faring nor in ships; [650] for never yet have I sailed by ship over the wide sea, but only to Euboea from Aulis where the Achaeans once stayed through much storm when they had gathered a great host from divine Hellas for Troy, the land of fair women. [655] Then I crossed over to Chalcis, to the games of wise Amphidamas where the sons of the great-hearted hero proclaimed and appointed prizes. And there I boast that I gained the victory with a song and carried off a handled tripod which I dedicated to the Muses of Helicon, in the place where they first set me in the way of clear song. [660] Such is all my experience of many-pegged ships; nevertheless I will tell you the will of Zeus who holds the aegis; for the Muses have taught me to sing in marvellous song. Fifty days after the solstice,[1] when the season of wearisome heat is come to an end, [665] is the right time for men to go sailing. Then you will not wreck your ship, nor will the sea destroy the sailors, unless Poseidon the Earth-Shaker be set upon it, or Zeus, the king of the deathless gods, wish to slay them; for the issues of good and evil alike are with them. [670] At that time the winds are steady, and the sea is harmless. Then trust in the winds without care, and haul your swift ship down to the sea and put all the freight on board; but make all haste you can to return home again and do not wait till the time of the new wine and autumn rain and [675] oncoming storms with the fierce gales of Notus who accompanies the heavy autumn rain of Zeus and stirs up the sea and makes the deep dangerous.

1 July-August.

Lines 678-705

Another time for men to go sailing is in spring when a man first sees leaves on the topmost shoot of a fig-tree as large as the foot-print that a crow makes; [680] then the sea is passable, and this is the spring sailing time. For my part I do not praise it, for my heart does not like it. Such a sailing is snatched, and you will hardly avoid mischief. Yet in their ignorance [685] men do even this, for wealth means life to poor mortals; but it is fearful to die among the waves. But I bid you consider all these things in your heart as I say. Do not put all your goods in hollow ships; [690] leave the greater part behind, and put the lesser part on board; for it is a bad business to meet with disaster among the waves of the sea, as it is bad if you put too great a load on your wagon and break the axle, and your goods are spoiled. Observe due measure: and proportion is best in all things. [695] Bring home a wife to your house when you are of the right age, while you are not far short of thirty years nor much above; this is the right age for marriage. Let your wife have been grown up four years, and marry her in the fifth. Marry a maiden, so that you can teach her careful ways, [700] and especially marry one who lives near you, but look well about you and see that your marriage will not be a joke to your neighbors. For a man wins nothing better than a good wife, and, again, nothing worse than a bad one, a greedy soul who [705] roasts her man without fire, strong though he may be, and brings him to a raw[1] old age.

1 *I.e.* untimely, premature. Juvenal similarly speaks of "cruda senectus" (caused by gluttony)

Lines 706-736

Be careful to avoid the anger of the deathless gods. Do not make a friend equal to a brother; but if you do, do not wrong him first, and do not lie to please the tongue. But if he wrongs you first, [710] offending either in word or in deed, remember to repay him double; but if he asks you to be his friend again and be ready to give you satisfaction, welcome him. He is a worthless man who makes now one and now another his friend; but as for you, do not let your face put your heart to shame.[1] [715] Do not get a name either as lavish or as churlish, as a friend of rogues, or as a slanderer of good men. Never dare to taunt a man with deadly poverty which eats out the heart; it is sent by the deathless gods. [720] The best treasure a man can have is a sparing tongue, and the greatest pleasure, one that moves orderly; for if you speak evil, you yourself will soon be worse spoken of. Do not be boorish at a common feast where there are many guests; the pleasure is greatest and the expense is least.[2] Never pour a libation of sparkling wine to Zeus after dawn [725] with unwashed hands, nor to others of the deathless gods; otherwise they do not hear your prayers but spit them back. Do not stand upright facing the sun when you make water, but remember to do this when he has set and towards his rising. And do not make water as you go, whether on the road or off the road, [730] and do not uncover yourself: the nights belong to the blessed gods. A scrupulous man who has a wise heart sits down or goes to the wall of an enclosed court. Do not expose yourself befouled by the fireside in your house, but avoid this. [735] Do not beget children when you are come back from ill-omened burial, but after a festival of the gods.

1 The thought is parallel to that of "O, what a goodly outside falsehood hath."

2 The "common feast" is one to which all present subscribe. Theognis (line 495) says that one of the chief pleasures of a banquet is the general conversation. Hence the present passage means that such a feast naturally costs little, while the many present will make pleasurable conversation.

Lines 737-764

Never cross the sweet-flowing water of ever-rolling rivers afoot until you have prayed, gazing into the soft flood, and washed your hands in the clear, lovely water. [740] Whoever crosses a river with hands unwashed of wickedness, the gods are angry with him and bring trouble upon him afterwards. At a cheerful festival of the gods do not cut the withered from the quick upon that which has five branches[1] with bright steel. Never put the ladle upon the mixing-bowl [745] at a wine party, for malignant ill-luck is attached to that. When you are building a house, do not leave it rough hewn, or a cawing crow may settle on it and croak. Take nothing to eat or to wash with from uncharmed pots, for in them there is mischief. [750] Do not let a boy of twelve years sit on things which may not be moved,[2] for that is bad, and makes a man unmanly; nor yet a child of twelve months, for that has the same effect. A man should not clean his body with water in which a woman has washed, for there is bitter mischief in that also for a time. [755] When you come upon a burning sacrifice, do not make a mock of mysteries, for Heaven is angry at this also. Never make water in the mouths of rivers which flow to the sea, nor yet in springs; but be careful to avoid this. And do not ease yourself in them: it is not well to do this. [760] So do: and avoid the talk of men. For Talk is mischievous, light, and easily raised, but hard to bear and difficult to be rid of. Talk never wholly dies away when many people voice her: even Talk is in some ways divine.

1 *I.e.*"do not cut your finger-nails."

2 *I.e.*things which it would be sacrilege to disturb, such as tombs.

Lines 765-799

Mark the days which come from Zeus, duly telling your slaves of them, and that the thirtieth day of the month is best for one to look over the work and to deal out supplies. [769] For these are days which come from Zeus the all-wise, [768] when men discern aright. [769] To begin with, the first, the fourth, and the seventh— [770] on which Leto bore Apollo with the blade of gold—each is a holy day. The eighth and the ninth, two days at least of the waxing month,[1] are especially good for the works of man. Also the eleventh and twelfth are both excellent, [775] alike for shearing sheep and for reaping the kindly fruits; but the twelfth is much better than the eleventh, for on it the airy-swinging spider spins its web in full day, and then the Wise One,[2] gathers her pile. On that day a woman should set up her loom and get forward with her work. [780] Avoid the thirteenth of the waxing month for beginning to sow: yet it is the best day for setting plants. The sixth of the mid-month is very unfavorable for plants, but is good for the birth of males, though unfavorable for a girl either to be born at all or to be married. [785] Nor is the first sixth a fit day for a girl to be born, but a kindly for gelding kids and sheep and for fencing in a sheep cote. It is favorable for the birth of a boy, but such will be fond of sharp speech, lies, cunning words, and stealthy conversation. [790] On the eighth of the month geld the boar and loud-bellowing bull, but hard-working mules on the twelfth. On the great twentieth, in full day, a wise man should be born. Such a one is very sound-witted. The tenth is favorable for a male to be born; but, for a girl, the fourth day [795] of the mid-month. On that day tame sheep and shambling, horned oxen, and the sharp-fanged dog and hardy mules to the touch of the hand. But take care to avoid troubles which eat out the heart on the fourth of the beginning and ending of the month; it is a day very fraught with fate.

1 The month is divided into three periods, the waxing, the mid-month, and the waning, which answer to the phases of the moon.

2 *I.e.* the ant

Lines 800-End

On the fourth of the month bring home your bride, but choose the omens which are best for this business. Avoid fifth days: they are unkindly and terrible. On a fifth, they say, the Erinyes assisted at the birth of Horcus (Oath) whom Eris (Strife) bore to trouble the forsworn. [805] Look about you very carefully and throw out Demeter's holy grain upon the well-rolled[1] threshing floor on the seventh of the mid-month. Let the woodman cut beams for house building and plenty of ships' timbers, such as are suitable for ships. On the fourth day begin to build narrow ships. [810] The ninth of the mid-month improves towards evening; but the first ninth of all is quite harmless for men. It is a good day on which to beget or to be born both for a male and a female: it is never a wholly evil day. Again, few know that the twenty-seventh of the month is best [815] for opening a wine jar, and putting yokes on the necks of oxen and mules and swift-footed horses, and for hauling a swift ship of many thwarts down to the sparkling sea; few call it by its right name. On the fourth day open a jar. The fourth of the mid-month is a day holy above all. And again, few men know that the fourth day after the twentieth is best while it is morning: [820] towards evening it is less good. These days are a great blessing to men on earth; but the rest are changeable, luckless, and bring nothing. Everyone praises a different day but few know their nature. Sometimes a day is a stepmother, sometimes a mother. [825] That man is happy and lucky in them who knows all these things and does his work without offending the deathless gods, who discerns the omens of birds and avoids transgression.

1 Such seems to be the meaning here, though the epithet is otherwise rendered "well-rounded." Corn was threshed by means of a sleigh with two runners having three or four rollers between them, like the modern Egyptian *nurag.*

Printed in Great Britain
by Amazon.co.uk, Ltd.,
Marston Gate.